Bizet's *Carmen* is probably the best known opera of the standard repertoire, yet its very familiarity often prevents us from approaching it with the seriousness it deserves. This handbook explores the opera in a number of contexts, bringing to the surface the controversies over gender, race, class and musical propriety that greeted its premiere and that have been rekindled by the recent spate of *Carmen* films. Beginning with a study of Mérimée's story *Carmen* by Peter Robinson and an examination of the social tensions in nineteenth-century France that inform both that story and the opera, the book traces the opera through its genesis and its various moments of reception, from its opening night to the present. Because *Carmen* is extremely eclectic, the diverse musical languages Bizet exploited for its composition (conventions of *opéra-comique*, German influences, codes developed for the representation of "the exotic") are investigated as well. The central core of the book presents a close reading of the opera that offers many new interpretive possibilities. The handbook concludes with discussions of four films based on the opera: *Carmen Jones* and the versions of *Carmen* by Carlos Saura, Peter Brook and Francesco Rosi.

The volume contains a bibliography, music examples, and a synopsis, and will be of interest to students, scholars and opera-goers.

CAMBRIDGE OPERA HANDBOOKS

Cambridge Opera Handbooks

Georges Bizet
Carmen

Poster by Leray for the first performance
(Reproduced courtesy of the Bibliothèque Nationale, Paris)

Georges Bizet
Carmen

SUSAN McCLARY
Professor of Musicology
University of Minnesota

CAMBRIDGE
UNIVERSITY PRESS

Published by the Press Syndicate of the University of Cambridge
The Pitt Building, Trumpington Street, Cambridge CB2 1RP
40 West 20th Street, New York, NY 10011–4211, USA
10 Stamford Road, Oakleigh, Victoria 3166, Australia

First published 1992

Printed and bound in Great Britain by
Woolnough Bookbinding Ltd, Irthlingborough, Northamptonshire

A catalogue record for this book is available from the British Library

Library of Congress cataloguing in publication data

McClary, Susan.
    Georges Bizet, Carmen / Susan McClary.
        p.   cm. – (Cambridge opera handbooks)
    Includes bibliographical references and index.
    ISBN 0 521 39301 9. – ISBN 0 521 39897 5 (pbk.)
    1. Bizet, Georges, 1838–75. Carmen. I. Title. II. Title:
Carmen. III. Series.
ML410.B62M25 1992
782.1–dc20   91–32840   CIP

ISBN 0 521 39301 9 hardback
ISBN 0 521 39897 5 paperback

CE

In memory of my father, Dan O. McClary

In memory of my father David C. Maloney

Contents

General preface

This is a series of studies of individual operas, written for the
serious opera-goer or record-collector as well as the student or
scholar. Each volume has three main concerns. The first is historical: to describe the genesis of the work, its sources or its relation
to literary prototypes, the collaboration between librettist and
composer, and the first performance and subsequent stage history.
This history is itself a record of changing attitudes towards the
work, and an index of general changes of taste. The second is
analytical and it is grounded in a very full synopsis which considers
the opera as a structure of musical and dramatic effects. In most
volumes there is also a musical analysis of a section of the score,
showing how the music serves or makes the drama. The analysis,
like the history, naturally raises questions of interpretation, and the
third concern of each volume is to show how critical writing about
an opera, like production and performance, can direct or distort
appreciation of its structural elements. Some conflict of interpretation is an inevitable part of this account; editors of the handbooks
reflect this – by citing classic statements, by commissioning new
essays, by taking up their own critical position. A final section gives
a select bibliography, a discography and guides to other sources.

1 *Mérimée's* Carmen

PETER ROBINSON

To the average reader of 1845, there was nothing particularly original or surprising about Prosper Mérimée's *Carmen* when it first appeared on October 1 in *La Revue des deux mondes*. It is, indeed, entirely possible that few recognized the story as fiction. *La Revue des deux mondes* (*Review of the Two Worlds*) had originally been founded as a bi-weekly travel journal depicting, for the civilized "world" of France, exotic landscapes and adventures in what today we call the Third World. The volume of October 1 contains Mérimée's contribution as lead with no indication of its nature, together with an article on Belgium and the Catholic Party since 1830, a literary/historical article on the satires of Lucilius, an article on the political situation in Germany in 1845, a synopsis of the political events of the previous fifteen days and a review of the historical plays of G. Revere. In this context, *Carmen* takes on all the trappings of a "Letter from Abroad." Not even professional critics appeared to notice the story.[1]

For several decades, French culture had manifested a fascination with history: the desire to rediscover the truths of the past, to place France at the head of a continuum of scientific progress, to assert its supremacy over lesser cultures. As we shall see in Chapter 3, this agenda was coupled with a fascination with the exotic, the bizarre and the supernatural, often resulting in stories very much like *Carmen*: stories in which a sober, high-minded French narrator, representative of French superiority and civilization, visits an area alien to him and reports upon what he finds. The events reported will always in one way or another surpass those he could live himself as a rational, dispassionate Frenchman.

In the case of *Carmen*, a scholarly, amateur French archaeologist has gone to Spain to locate the real battlefield of Munda, the location where Caesar finally defeated the Republican forces in the Roman Civil War. This quest is interrupted by a series of events so interesting that they delay his telling us of his discoveries, postponing them to a later time and another text. While looking for the battlefield, the narrator comes across a real Spanish bandit, a wonderful, exotic specimen he has for years hoped to meet. Using his superior French skills, the narrator succeeds in taming and observing this wild beast and discovers in him a rather sympathetic human being named Don José. The narrator helps the beast to escape from the authorities and continues his journey. He arrives in Cordoba and there meets another specimen he has hoped to study – the fortune-telling gypsy. Again he is beguiled by his observations, this time of none other than Carmen herself, and he manages to repair with her to her rooms for the telling of his fortune and other delights. What he might have learned is interrupted by Don José, and the Frenchman is forced to continue his travels. When he returns to Cordoba several months later, he finds Don José in prison condemned to die for having killed Carmen. Don José relates his own story, and this concludes the first version of the tale.

Late in 1846 Mérimée added a fourth section to what had been a three-part story, puzzling readers and critics alike. In this fourth section, the French narrator returns and delivers a long-winded disquisition on Romany, the gypsy language – its origins, its dialects, its influence on French slang, its qualities and its proverbs. He ends this part and thus the entire story by quoting a gypsy proverb: "*En retudi panda nasti abela macha*," which he translates as "En close bouche n'entre point mouche" (p. 409); "Into a closed mouth enters no fly").

On the surface, then, we are faced with a commonplace: two exotic anecdotes – predictably dealing with the uncivilized and thus, stereotypically, the violent, the disorderly, the superstitious, the diabolical – sandwiched in the middle of the narrator's discourse, which is composed of order, rationality, logic, that is to say, the hallmarks of French civilization. Were this to constitute the interest of the story, perhaps little would be thought of it today. After all, so many stories of the period have precisely the same construction. Yet within several years of its publication, people were beginning to notice the story, to consider it one of Mérimée's best – indeed, to call it a masterpiece. This was true even before Bizet was to catapult a version of it into worldwide notoriety some thirty years after the original was written. We must therefore look further in the attempt to discover the reasons for the powerful hold this tale has had on readers up to the present day.

Virtually all of the elements that compose the structure of the story are intimately linked to questions of control and mastery, as the major narrative strategy aptly illustrates. A Frenchman begins the story with learned, controlled discourse about history and local color, then surrenders his control to another tale told by a different narrator (foreign, violent, uncivilized). This tale takes over the French text and at least temporarily entirely subverts its control. Violence erupts, forcing the Frenchman to reassert mastery. He does so by attempting to reweave the torn fabric with yet another learned discourse, this time upon the nature of language in general, and of Romany in particular. It is precisely the gypsy language that was ostensibly obliterated with Carmen's death but that now has been appropriated by the Frenchman. He demonstrates his mastery and control by showing us a thoroughly domesticated tongue silenced finally when he, according to his own desires, chooses to cease writing.

The paradigm of control and subsequent threat to its hegemony is echoed throughout the text by any number of the episodes and anecdotes that compose it – the threat to Caesar's control by the Republicans; the fact that Don José himself is a member of an occupying army charged with keeping the local population in check; the smugglers' defiance of commercial law, and so on. Interestingly, as the story unfolds and one perceives these threats to control, one begins to notice that blame for almost all of the threats is attributed to Carmen herself. Her action in the cigar factory forces the army to impose order; her mockery leads Don José to disobey his duty to return to his barracks; her efforts free her husband from rightful imprisonment; her schemes organize the band of smugglers. Finally, her resistance to Don José is blamed for the ultimate assertion of power and control – the violence resulting in her death. Indeed, Carmen is everywhere and even spills out of the frame meant to contain her, as she seduces not only the foreign and violent narrator but the rational French narrator as well. Herein lies the obsession of the text. It always returns to Carmen; indeed, the tale begins at the name itself.

The linguistic mystification of at least some readers also begins immediately. The meaning of the word "Carmen" would not be readily decipherable to the reader of the time, as it is not a French word and would only become immediately recognizable as a proper name after this very story had become famous.[2] This mystification deepens as the reader's eyes fall next upon a text not in French but in Greek. The epigraph is a quotation from the Greek author Palladas. Male readers in Mérimée's day could be expected to be able to read Greek, since instruction in the language was part of their education. Women readers, however, did not receive the same education, and most of them could not have discerned that it is they who are at issue in the epigraph: "Every woman is bitter as bile, but each has two good moments, one in bed and the other in the grave."[3]

The reader is thus immediately faced with another example of the drive for control. At the very outset of the story – in the title and the epigraph – the reader is notified that progress and understanding are impossible without the intervention of a master translator. Only he possesses the key to unlock the secrets of the many languages that might be used (and no fewer than seven languages are invoked in *Carmen* – Basque, English, French, Greek, Romany, Latin and Spanish). Significantly, the French narrator obligingly plays that role throughout the rest of the story, providing at least forty footnotes that translate expressions, explain details of local color or go so far as to elucidate metaphors whose meaning is obvious.

For the epigraph, however, Mérimée refuses to provide helpful information to female readers, thus at one and the same time telling men quite precisely what the story really concerns and occluding access to women. The battle that really interests this text is the battle between the sexes. From the very beginning, Woman is marked as the enemy. The battlefield itself, the territory that obsesses the text, is none other than her body, as the text constantly raises the question of who shall own it while describing those who are fighting over it.

The obsessional nature of this concern over the woman's body is apparent from the beginning of the story. The French narrator, while wandering around the plains looking for Munda, seeks a place to rest. His eyes light upon what can only be described as an uncannily feminine landscape. He is attracted to a spot of moisture and, approaching it, discovers a small stream trickling through high, narrow foothills. He resolves to penetrate this space in hopes of finding better within. Sure enough, the narrow gorge opens suddenly on to a natural space shaded by the high walls surrounding it. In the center of this uterine place is found a spring, the entirety causing the narrator to exclaim:

Il était impossible de rencontrer un lieu qui promît au voyageur une halte plus agréable. Au pied de rochers à pic, la source s'élançait en bouillonnant et tombait dans un petit bassin tapissé d'un sable blanc comme la neige. Cinq à six beaux chênes verts, toujours à l'abri du vent et rafraîchis par la source, s'élevaient sur ses bords, et la couvraient de leur épais ombrage; enfin, autour du bassin,[4] une herbe fine, lustrée, offrait un lit meilleur qu'on n'en eût trouvé dans aucune auberge à dix lieues à la ronde. (p. 346)

(It was impossible to encounter a spot that promised the traveler a more agreeable halt. At the foot of vertiginous rocks the spring boiled out and fell into a little basin carpeted with a sand white as snow. Five or six oaks, always sheltered from the wind and refreshed by the spring, rose on its borders, and covered it with their heavy shade; finally, around the basin, a fine, lustrous grass offered a bed better than could be found in any inn within a radius of ten leagues.)

Regrettably for the narrator this body he has penetrated is already occupied, for it is here that he meets Don José, who is quite prepared to defend his territory with the blunderbuss he holds conveniently out from his side. Realizing that he has nothing to match the blunderbuss, the Frenchman approaches, bows to *force majeure* and offers up what he can – namely, a cigar. There ensues an extraordinary scene of male bonding in which Don José lights his cigar off the Frenchman's, they breathe smoke together and the narrator carefully explains that in Spain this establishes a link of hospitality. The link established, the two men share food and ultimately lie down together to sleep. When the Frenchman learns his new friend is to be arrested, the demands of this companionship require the abandonment of the principles of law. He wakens Don José and warns him of his impending capture.

The most important consequence of this scene is to abolish any real difference that might have existed between the civilized, distant Frenchman and the wild, Spanish bandit. They are now essentially brothers, each like the other and in some sense each responsible for the other. Certainly the Frenchman feels this strongly as he debates with himself whether or not he should have done what he did:

Je me demandais si j'avais eu raison de sauver de la potence un voleur, et peut-être un meurtrier, et cela seulement parce que j'avais mangé avec lui du jambon et du riz à la valencienne. N'avais-je pas trahi mon guide, qui soutenait la cause des lois; ne l'avais-je pas exposé à la vengeance d'un scélérat? Mais les devoirs de l'hospitalité? ... Préjugé de sauvage, me disais-je; j'aurai à répondre de tous les crimes que le bandit va commettre

... Pourtant est-ce un préjugé que cet instinct de conscience qui résiste à tous les raisonnements? (p. 356)

(I wondered if I had been right to save a robber from the gallows, and perhaps a murderer, and this only because I had eaten ham and rice *à la valencienne* with him. Had I not betrayed my guide, who was upholding the cause of law; had I not exposed him to the revenge of a scoundrel? But the duties of hospitality? ... Prejudice of the barbaric, I said to myself; I will have to answer for all the crimes the bandit will commit ... Yet is it a prejudice, this instinct of conscience that resists all reasoning?)

"Cet instinct de conscience" is both the result and cause of male bonding. Held together now by something stronger than societal judgments concerning law and order, or other abstract moral principles, these two men are now brothers-in-arms, fighting the same battles and enduring the same vicissitudes. The acts of the one are to be considered the acts of the other.

The relation between men and women is explored shortly afterward. Here, instead of linkage and bonding, is found difference and alienation. While in Cordoba, the Frenchman hears and tells about a curious activity of the women. At nightfall, just as the *angelus* rings out its last note, the women of the town gather together on the banks of the Guadalquivir River. Believing themselves protected by the cover of night, they disrobe and bathe in the river, unmindful of the men. The men, excited by the prospect of such a feast of flesh, gather on the high embankment of the river and stare excitedly into the water. They have even been known to bribe the bell-ringer so that the *angelus* will sound during a time of light, facilitating the seeing of these beauties. The Frenchman regretfully points out that the bell-ringers are today incorruptible, and distinguishing between the oldest hag and the youngest beauty is not really possible. The men remain on the periphery of this female world, forced to sublimate their desires voyeuristically: "Cependant, ces formes blanches et incertaines qui se dessinent sur le sombre azur du fleuve font travailler les esprits poétiques, et, avec un peu d'imagination, il n'est pas difficile de se représenter Diane et ses nymphes au bain, sans avoir à craindre le sort d'Actéon" (p. 357; "However, these white and uncertain forms which stand out against the dark blue of the river set poetic minds to work, and, with a little imagination, it is not difficult to see Diana and her nymphs bathing, without having to fear Actaeon's fate"). What is of interest to them is solely the physical aspect of the female – the women's bodies are their focus.[5] The evocation of Diana is particularly telling. By remaining outside the woman's world, the tremulous male is left to be satisfied by fantasy alone, thus protecting him from the dangers of real, physical contact with the women who – like Diana – seem quite capable of destroying him.

This fear of destruction by the female is immediately illustrated by the Frenchman's encounter with Carmen. Participating in the *angelus* bathing scene one night, he finds himself face to face with a woman. There follows a reenactment of the bonding scene with Don José, but to quite different effect. The woman allows her mantilla to slide off her shoulder, thus revealing her weapon – her flesh. While a moment before the Frenchman could see nothing, now he immediately sees her as enticing, young and with big eyes. His first act is to throw away his cigar, thereby disarming himself. She, however, claims that she likes cigar smoke and even likes to smoke little cigars herself. He just happens to have some in a case, which he opens for her. They then smoke together. Again the Frenchman offers food as a sequel, this time inviting Carmen to accompany him for ice cream. Before agreeing, she asks him the time. "Je fis sonner ma montre" (p. 358; "I had my watch strike") is his response. Taking his watch from his vest pocket, he allows it to ring out his prowess, at which she marvels. Later she again asks the time, and he again sounds it out.

As the seduction unfolds, the two proceed from the public square to increasingly private spaces, finally ending in Carmen's room where the Frenchman believes he is about to conquer. At the moment of culmination, however, the door bursts open and Don José enters. In an exact replay of the earlier scene in the mountains, two men now face each other, contending for ascendancy over a body. Here, instead of a sublimated, fantasized female landscape, we are faced with Carmen's body, and here the tensions are much higher. The Frenchman senses that she is urging Don José to kill him, and he wishes that he had allowed Don José to be arrested. The conclusion seems inescapable that women, or at least this woman, constitute the greatest threat to the bond that exists between men.

Luckily Don José manages to resist, the tension is deflected and he escorts the Frenchman to safety. He knows what the Frenchman does not – that the visitor was about to be ensnared, that the Frenchman would have become Carmen's victim as Don José had already become. Don José could now repay his debt and save the Frenchman's life by leading him out of the maze of Carmen's world. When the Frenchman returns to his own room, he notes: "Le pire fut qu'en me déshabillant je m'aperçus que ma montre me manquait" (p. 363; "The worst was that while undressing I noticed my watch was missing"). Diana/Carmen has found him out and robbed him of his prowess. The result, then, of this episode is not like its male counterpart, one of friendship, bond and solidarity, but rather the opposite. It demonstrates mistrust, guile and alienation.

It is here that the narration is taken over by Don José. By now, however, it is clear that it does not matter. The vaunted superiority of the rational, civilized Frenchman has been reduced to the same level as Don José. In a very real sense what happens to Don José is the responsibility of the Frenchman, not just because he allowed Don José to escape, but because he and Don José are just alike. Both men instinctively see the other as a brother, and each sees himself as the victim of the same woman who has robbed them both. The dispassionate, distant Frenchman who knows the classics and can quote Greek has exactly the same attitude toward women as the Spaniard who overtly fears them. There is no longer the need for any pretense: the ancient Greeks, the civilized French, the exotic Spanish – all men have the same story to tell.

On the surface the story plays out in stereotypical fashion. Both the Frenchman and Don José see Carmen as a manifestation of the devil. For the Frenchman she is a gypsy, thus marked from the beginning with alterity. She is the lowest form of human life possible, even lower than the Jew he believes her to be when he first sees her (although, as we shall see, he cannot bring himself to utter the name "Jew"). As her charms are those of Satan himself, both men are helpless and cannot be held responsible for their actions. Everything she ostensibly wants them to do – lie, cheat, steal, revolt – they cannot refuse. They are her victims. Carmen tells Don José that he should leave her because certainly she will cause him to be hanged. But, of course, she has bewitched him so he cannot. Killing her, then, becomes a last act of desperation, the act necessary to reassert order and control. He is to be pitied; she is to be blamed. Surely this is how the story has been read over the years.

Yet it is not at all clear that Carmen really deserves to be blamed for what happens. Don José's propensity for violence is established well before he meets Carmen. His killing of another Basque in Navarre, which necessitated his going to Andalusia, already marks him a murderer. Moreover, Carmen warns him repeatedly that he should have nothing to do with her as he is too naïve and stupid to be able to handle someone like her. He, of course, refuses to listen.

Close reading of the text uncovers a portrait of Carmen that has nothing to do with the satanic: she is granted characteristics that in other circumstances would have been seen as laudable and, indeed, particularly male. The "crime" for which she was arrested, slashing the face of another woman, would not have been seen as a crime if committed by a male. Carmen's honor and integrity were impugned by the other woman who accused Carmen of being a whore. Like any man – French or Spanish – Carmen reacted with vigor and immediately defended herself with her weapon. Mérimée himself was well known for his quickness to take offense, his propensity for dueling.

After she is arrested, she too uses a technique of bonding – speaking the same language as her captor – to escape. Feeling that a bond has been established, that she has a debt to pay for Don José's allowing her to go free, she at first attempts to pay it in her own currency. The French narrator points out several times in the work that gypsies prize their freedom above all else. Carmen thus sends Don José a loaf of bread containing a file and money to allow him to escape from prison. He refuses this offer, as it goes counter to his own sense of honor and duty. Carmen therefore changes this currency to one she knows Don José will appreciate. She invites him to the tavern of Lillas Pastia and there sleeps with him.

For Don José, however, the preferred medium of exchange is possession, not liberty. Here lies the most fundamental misunderstanding between the two. What Carmen gives freely in order to repay what she considers an obligation she clearly believes frees her from obligation. Don José, however, takes her act as a sign that he now owns Carmen and that she is obligated to him in perpetuity. The morning after, Carmen considers there is nothing more between them, as she says: "Ecoute, Joseito, t'ai-je payé? D'après notre loi, je ne te devais rien, puisque tu es un *payllo*; mais tu es un joli garçon et tu m'as plu. Nous sommes quittes. Bonjour" (p. 379; "Listen, Joseito, have I paid you? According to our law I owed you nothing since you are a *payllo* [a foreigner]; but you are a handsome boy and you pleased me. We are quits. Goodbye"). He, however, does not get the point and immediately wants to set up another assignation. Several weeks later, when Don José is guarding a breach in the town wall from smugglers, Carmen approaches him and offers to pay him to allow her smuggling friends to get through.

He refuses, outraged. She then offers to pay with her body and again he refuses, but unhappily. As she turns to make the offer elsewhere he capitulates. The dynamics of this scene are repeated many times in the story. Every time Carmen wishes to get her way, to do so she is forced to use her body with the men who hold the power. Increasingly she resents it.

Carmen is not only endowed with great physical attractiveness, but is also described in the story as having the power and dedication to heal. During a duel with his lieutenant – which Carmen urges Don José not to get into – Don José is wounded. Carmen and a friend clean the wound, hide Don José from the authorities and, with special medicines, nurse him back to health. Later Carmen again saves Don José's life. He has been wounded when his band of smugglers is caught by the police, and he crawls away to die. Carmen finds him and, over a long period of time, nurses him back to health. What is extraordinary about this scene is that it takes place long after Carmen has ceased loving Don José, and his possessiveness and jealousy have made her life miserable. She, however, never abandons someone in need and is never herself violent.

Finally, it must be pointed out that Carmen is the most intelligent person in the story. It is she who manages to free her husband from jail, and it is she who organizes all of the escapades of the band of smugglers. She is its *de facto* leader, thinking up the schemes whereby it can succeed, marshaling the troops of the band throughout the countryside, managing large amounts of money and numbers of contingencies in her head. The band simply could not exist without her. Everyone else in it is replaceable except Carmen. Curiously she combines all the male virtues: she is clever, intelligent, brave, resolute, sexual, independent. Why then is she so despised, so threatening that she must be destroyed?

The most obvious threat is Carmen's sexuality. The text is obsessed by her physicality, her body and its movements. Virtually every time she appears at the beginning of the story, she reveals her flesh. The Frenchman narrator cannot make out her features at night until she removes her mantilla from her shoulders. Then suddenly he sees clearly that she is young, well-built ("bien faite") and has large eyes. Precisely the same movement attracts Don José, and he is subsequently transfixed by the movement of her body and by the sight of the flesh of her legs pushing through holes in her stockings.

While all this flesh is powerfully attractive, what is more important is the sense of inadequacy it engenders in the men. The text is obsessed with images of male inadequacy faced with such allurement. Even the most reluctant freudian must recognize the extraordinary number of phallic images used to characterize the males in the story. When the reader first encounters Don José, he is standing in the earlier-described feminine landscape with a raised blunderbuss. The Frenchman, seeing such endowment, immediately surrenders his cigars. Subsequently we learn in Don José's narrative that he had started off with a *maquilla*, a long walking stick-like instrument with an iron head.

Moreover, Don José's first colloquy with Carmen is a series of obscene *doubles entendres*. While mounting guard, Don José occupies himself with fashioning a chain of wool to attach his *épinglette*, the little needle used to ream out the touchhole of his blunderbuss. Carmen suggests that he should use the chain to hold the keys to her strongbox and then goes on to declare that since he only has a needle he must be a lacemaker – namely, a woman. Clearly, neither the thin woolen string nor the little needle are sufficient to secure her strongbox. Later she cajoles Don José by saying that the Andalusians with their knives are no match for the Basques and their *maquillas*. When the French narrator first meets Carmen, he immediately throws away his cigar and replaces it with a *papelito*. Note that both the *épinglette* and the *papelito* are diminutives. And the Frenchman only observes when he is undressed that he has been robbed of his watch by none other than Carmen. Need one point out that in the cigar factory Carmen's job is to cut off the ends of the cigars?

Initially, when fighting other men, Don José possesses either a blunderbuss or saber, but he progressively seems to lose them and is reduced when fighting Carmen's husband to using a knife. As he kills the husband, Don José's knife breaks, and he assumes the knife of the husband. It is with this appropriated instrument that he kills Carmen. What is most curious is that Don José uses this very knife to dig Carmen's grave – in quite rocky soil. This is a most inadequate instrument for the task, particularly in a story which prides itself upon its realistic detail.

There remains the puzzling fourth section added less than a year after the first version was published. To most readers and critics this section remains enigmatic and disappointing. The various reasons adduced for its existence are unconvincing,[6] and many critics simply leave it unmentioned. Proper study and understanding of the fourth section is, however, crucial. The issue of control and domination is engaged by the French narrator primarily through language itself. It is he who is to be seen as the interpreter: the one who can go into a foreign land, manipulate its language or languages and provide the necessary understanding to the reader who does not command so many tongues. That he is as willing to conceal as to reveal is evidenced by his refusal to translate the Greek epigraph at the beginning of the story.

The Frenchman narrator's initial analysis of others is through a commentary on their manner of speaking. He says of Don José, "C'étaient les premiers mots qu'il faisait entendre, et je remarquai qu'il ne prononçait pas l'*s* à la manière andalouse, d'où je conclus que c'était un voyageur comme moi, moins archéologue seulement" (p. 348; "These were the first words he spoke, and I noticed that he did not pronounce the *s* in the Andalusian manner, from which I concluded that he was a voyager like me, only less archaeological"). Not only does this Frenchman know Spanish, he knows it well. When later he asks Don José to sing, he recognizes that the words are not Spanish but Basque. Our civilized, rational narrator is an expert linguist who prides himself on his knowledge and analytic powers.

When this same rational Frenchman meets Carmen, his powers utterly desert him. While the scene is somewhat long, it is significant. After the Frenchman and Carmen smoke together and she asks him for the time, the following exchange takes place:

– Quelles inventions on a chez vous, messieurs les étrangers! De quel pays êtes-vous, monsieur? Anglais, sans doute? – Français et votre grand serviteur. Et vous, mademoiselle, ou madame, vous êtes sans doute de Cordoue? – Non. – Vous êtes du moins Andalouse. Il me semble le reconnaître à votre doux parler. – Si vous remarquez si bien l'accent du monde, vous devez bien deviner qui je suis. – Je crois que vous êtes du pays de Jésus, à deux pas du paradis. (J'avais appris cette métaphore, qui désigne l'Andalousie, de mon ami Francisco Sevilla, *picador* bien connu.) – Bah! le paradis . . . les gens d'ici disent qu'il n'est pas fait pour nous. – Alors, vous seriez donc moresque, ou . . . je m'arrêtai, n'osant dire juive. – Allons, allons! vous voyez bien que je suis bohémienne; voulez-vous que je vous dise *la baji*? Avez-vous entendu parler de la Carmencita? C'est moi. (p. 349)

(What inventions you have in your countries, you foreigners! What country are you from, sir? English, no doubt?/French and your servant.

And you, Miss, or Madam, you are doubtless from Cordoba?/No./You are at least Andalusian. I seem to recognize that from your soft way of speaking./If you recognize so readily the accent of the world, you should easily guess who I am./I believe that you are from the land of Jesus, two steps from paradise. (I had learned this metaphor, which designates Andalusia, from my friend Francisco Sevilla, a well-known *picador*.)/Bah! paradise . . . people from here say that it isn't made for us./Then you would be Moorish, or . . . I stopped, not daring to say Jewish./Come on, come on! You see perfectly well that I am gypsy; do you want me to tell your fortune? Have you heard of Carmencita? That's me.)

In this extraordinary scene, not only is the narrator ignorant, he is tongue-tied. Carmen's use of language so far surpasses his knowledge that he cannot place it or, as a consequence, her. He insists first that she is from the very town they are in, then, if not the town, at least its province. When that does not elicit the response desired he insists again, using a deeply ambiguous metaphor. By saying that she must be from the "land of Jesus," he can be referring not only to Andalusia as he claims, but also to Israel, the very category he dare not mention. For him Carmen is unnameable and in this respect is marked from the outset as monstrous. Indeed she is so monstrous she belongs to an even more alienated category than that of Jew, a category that does not even occur to the Frenchman – that of gypsy.

As Carmen surpasses Don José in the realm of the sexual, she equally surpasses our Frenchman in the realm of language. Her capacity to speak many languages and to speak them so well that she fools others is one element of her success in getting what she wants. Thus by speaking to Don José in Basque she manages to effect her escape. She is in fact the only character in the story who speaks all the vernacular languages invoked. The Frenchman does not know Romany, at least not in the first three sections of the story. When Carmen is talking to Don José in front of the Frenchman, she does so in Romany and the Frenchman cannot understand. Yet it is precisely at this moment in the story that his life is most directly threatened. Don José in his narration comments at some length upon the fact that gypsies, because they live everywhere, take on the language of wherever they are living, becoming *de facto* superb linguists.

The fourth section of the story now becomes quite pertinent. Don José's unwillingness to allow a woman who is superior to him both intellectually and sexually to remain independent and free*Recollections* from his domination is matched here by the Frenchman's equal inability. Carmen's skill in using languages unknown to the narrator himself threatens the very existence of the story itself, or at least of the narrator's version of the story. How can he master events if they are rendered in a language he cannot manipulate?

Once again we find no real difference between the rational, logical, civilized Frenchman and the wild, passionate, barbaric Don José. Both have been equally dominated and overwhelmed. The violent reassertion of order and dominance which is Don José's murder of Carmen is duplicated by the fourth section. Desperately trying to reassert his authority, the French narrator does violence to the very fabric of the story by now claiming to know a language he previously said he did not understand. Appropriating Carmen's language as Don José did her body, the Frenchman will finally finish her off, as well as end the threat she represents. Her language is now his and is completely tamed, dissected, analyzed.

The proverb with which the new story ends, "into closed mouth enters no fly," thus takes on a chilling meaning, for, after all, whose mouth has been closed? Writing over Carmen's language, the Frenchman attempts to write her off. Sealing every possible orifice, the sexual and the verbal, he brings the story to its end – silence. In this way he hopes forever to bury and to deny the terrifying reality of Woman's inalterable and unutterable superiority.[7]

2 *The genesis of Bizet's* Carmen

In 1872 the co-directors of the Opéra-Comique, Camille Du Locle and Adolphe de Leuven, approached Georges Bizet and proposed that he write an opera in collaboration with the librettists Ludovic Halévy and Henri Meilhac. De Leuven offered Bizet three scenarios as suggestions, but Bizet rejected them in favor of an idea to which he held tenaciously, even in the face of what became the severe opposition of his collaborators: he insisted that the new work be based on Mérimée's *Carmen*. From our vantage point, over a century after Bizet's *Carmen* triumphed as a masterpiece, we may have difficulty seeing his choice as problematic. But this choice contributed to de Leuven's decision to resign, provoked rebellions among the performers and incited the wrath of music critics before the public finally embraced Bizet's vision – unfortunately, only after his death.

During this period, France had two subsidized opera houses: the Opéra and the Opéra-Comique, which differed with respect to both target audience and musical genre. The Opéra commissioned and presented French Grand Opera to an upper-class clientele, while the Opéra-Comique specialized in the production of *opéras-comiques*, largely geared for a family-oriented bourgeoisie. A century earlier the genre of *opéra-comique* had been a vehicle for social satire, aimed in part at puncturing the stuffy conventions of elite operatic procedures. In place of lavish spectacle and uninterrupted singing, *opéras-comiques* featured a style that alternated lyrical expression with spoken dialogue, and they focused on more topical subject matter.

Gradually, however, the emphasis of *opéra-comique* changed. Under the guidance of impresarios such as de Leuven, its most prominent composers (for instance, Auber and Boieldieu) had developed narrative and musical formulas designed to satisfy an increasingly conservative audience. Indeed, the institution catered very self-consciously to betrothed couples and their cautious parents, a group that reliably provided at least twenty percent of box-office proceeds. By the 1850s, the conventions of the Opéra-Comique had become as rigid, its offerings as stagnant as those of the Opéra.

A few other important music-theater venues existed in Paris in the 1860s. In the operetta theaters, Offenbach's works exploited the element of social satire that the Opéra-Comique had gradually purged in the interest of good (conservative) taste. And the Théâtre-Lyrique, under the direction of Léon Carvalho, commissioned works of the *opéra-comique* genre that took greater risks than those produced by the Opéra-Comique. Gounod's *Faust* (1859) and two of Bizet's operas, *Les Pêcheurs de perles* (1863) and *La Jolie Fille de Perth* (1867), premiered at the Théâtre-Lyrique. But Carvalho's talents at administration failed to match his artistic discrimination, and his company folded in 1868.

In 1869 Du Locle was appointed co-director with de Leuven of the Opéra-Comique in an attempt at revitalizing that institution and attracting a wider audience, and during that same year he contacted Bizet about the possibility of writing a new work for the Opéra-Comique. If he had intended to call into question the very premises of his theater, he had come to the right place. Bizet had responded: "I shall be delighted to . . . try to change the *genre* of *opéra-comique*. Down with [Boieldieu's] *La Dame blanche!*"[1]

This first commission resulted in *Djamileh* (1872), an Orientalist fantasy that suited the taste for the exotic of both Bizet and Du Locle (later a collaborator and producer for *Aïda*). Even though neither public nor reviewers received *Djamileh* well, it impressed Du Locle sufficiently for him to commission a second work from Bizet. Bizet likewise felt that *Djamileh* succeeded in breaking new ground for him, despite its critical failure: "What gives me more satisfaction than the opinion of all these gentry is the absolute certainty of having found my path. I know what I am doing. I have just been ordered to compose three acts for the Opéra-Comique. Meilhac and Halévy are doing my piece. It will be *gay*, but with a gaiety that permits style."[2]

The defensive tone of this passage may surprise us, for we assume that Bizet knew what he was doing when embarking on this, his masterpiece. But neither he nor his colleagues had particular cause for optimism. After a promising start, which included the Prix de Rome, the protection of Gounod and the admiration of

Liszt for his piano virtuosity, Bizet still had not attained the degree of success or produced the quality of work that had been expected of him. Were it not for *Carmen*, Bizet's name would be no more familiar to us than those of his many contemporaries who were active in cultural production at the time but who are now forgotten.

Because of *Carmen*, however, musicologists have combed patiently through Bizet's earlier works in pursuit of traces of his genius and treasures that may have been unjustly neglected. The prestige of his name inspires occasional performances of some of his other works, but this would most certainly not be the case without *Carmen*. While his earlier compositions reveal competence and charm, they do not merit special attention, except through their authorial affiliation with *Carmen*. His record before 1872 warrants his defensiveness.

But if Bizet's earlier career boasts nothing comparable to his final work, it also indicates clearly that *Carmen* did not emerge from a vacuum. All his music bears the marks of his rigorous training at the Conservatoire, which steeped him in harmony, counterpoint and orchestration. His experience in music theater (as accompanist, apprentice, arranger, coach, composer of incidental music) instilled in him reservoirs of practical knowledge concerning stage production, performers and audiences. Even his years of "hack" work (churning out commercial arrangements for a living) contributed a high level of facility. And throughout his life, Bizet was attracted to many different musical discourses (opera of all genres, German symphonies, the popular songs and dances of the bohemian cabaret); without familiarity with all of these musics, he could not have created the vibrantly eclectic world of *Carmen*. His early work also displays a tendency to stretch generic boundaries, to resist convention.

Some of Bizet's earlier compositions herald rather more specifically certain aspects of *Carmen*. Several tunes known to us only from their *Carmen* incarnations appeared first in other contexts. Thus, Don José's outburst in Act III ("Dût-il m'en coûter la vie") is borrowed from *La Coupe du Roi de Thulé*, and his "Flower Song" appeared first in sketches for *Griséldis*. Micaëla's air, "Je dis que rien ne m'épouvante," may likewise have been composed for *Griséldis*.[3]

More important, certain thematic preoccupations evident throughout his career reach fruition in *Carmen*. First, Bizet was always drawn to exotic subject matter. To be sure, "Orientalism" was in vogue in France at this time, and few creative artists avoided it (see Chapter 3). But Bizet seems to have found it virtually impossible to compose without this stimulus. While his exotic locales varied (Russia, the Middle East, Brazil), they provided him the opportunity to indulge in music marked as "Other" with respect to Conservatoire norms.

Second, narratives involving the *femme fatale* and her innocent male victim reappear in many of his works, including *La Coupe du Roi de Thulé* (1869) and *L'Arlésienne* (1872). We need not rummage through Bizet's private life for explanations, for this too was a common obsession in late nineteenth-century culture (see Chapter 3). *Carmen* must be counted among the vast number of *femme fatale* stories produced during this period, even though Bizet treats the genre's stereotypes with far more subtlety and ambiguity than was usual.

In any case, when Du Locle invited him to write the opera that became *Carmen*, Bizet was primed for the task. The Opéra-Comique gave him the opportunity of working with the dramatists Meilhac and Halévy, who figured among the most successful men in the Parisian theater scene, especially the popular boulevard stage. As a team they had produced libretti for some of Offenbach's celebrated operettas (including *La Belle Hélène* and *La Vie parisienne*); when *Carmen* opened, they had four shows running simultaneously in Paris. Thus they brought to the collaboration with Bizet both name-recognition and theatrical experience, although they also brought associations with farce and vaudeville, rather than opera. Just before the premiere of *Carmen*, Halévy testified that the librettists regarded the opera as a side venture:

There are some very, very lovely and charming things in the score, and I dare hope for a happy evening for Bizet. His interests alone matter in this instance. The thing has little importance for Meilhac and me. If *Carmen* does open on Wednesday we shall have a *première* and a hundredth performance on the same night, *Carmen* and *La Boule*.[4]

In their collaborations, Meilhac wrote the prose dialogue, while Halévy provided the verse, and we can assume that this was the case with the libretto for *Carmen*. Meilhac's contributions are most obvious in the comic dialogues among the gypsies, for which there is no precedent in Mérimée. These disappear almost altogether in the recitative version of the opera produced by Ernest Guiraud after Bizet's death for the premiere in Vienna in October 1875.

Unfortunately, we find it necessary to assume or guess quite a bit concerning the genesis of *Carmen*, for few documents from the collaboration survive. This is true for two reasons. First, the artists were in close daily contact, and they seem to have transacted few of their deliberations in writing. Occasionally, a memoir records an important event, but these are quite haphazard. Second, the letters and diaries of Bizet and his family (including those of Ludovic Halévy, a cousin of Bizet's wife) for precisely this period were systematically censored after Bizet's death: that is, accounts of events were either blacked over or excised from the pages. For instance, Halévy began his entry for September 1, 1874 with "*Carmen* is in rehearsal at the Opéra-Comique," and the rest of the page is thoroughly obliterated.

The motivation for this severe mutilation of records remains unclear. Bizet's marriage was quite unstable during this period, and rumors of various sorts (some involving Bizet, others his wife) were circulating at the time. We can speculate about this situation, but are unlikely to find ultimate answers.[5] Regardless of the personal reasons leading to this state of affairs, it remains that for information concerning *Carmen*, we must rely on rehearsal log-books and recollections from participants in the original production as they were set down years later.

Some of our insights come from an engaging anecdotal account Halévy wrote in 1905, on the occasion of *Carmen*'s one-thousandth performance.[6] We must keep in mind, however, that he produced this report some thirty years after the events in question, that he had long before expunged his entries concerning the events from his daily journal, and that he composed this memoir while basking in the glory of *Carmen*'s unparalleled success.

All accounts concur that Bizet initiated the idea of adapting Mérimée's novella. Halévy recalls Meilhac, Du Locle and himself as extremely enthusiastic about this proposal, though Du Locle was apprehensive about de Leuven's probable reaction. According to Halévy, Du Locle said:

"But we have de Leuven to contend with. Such a subject would put him in a rage. He is very fond of you, Ludovic. Go see him. Perhaps you could convince him" ... I had not finished my first sentence when [de Leuven] interrupted: "Carmen! The Carmen of Mérimée? Wasn't she murdered by her lover? And the underworld of thieves, Gypsies, cigarette girls – at the Opéra-Comique, the theater of families, of wedding parties? You would put the public to flight. No, no, impossible!" (p. 36)

Halévy then recounts a negotiation process in which certain details involving the nature of the adaptation first become clear.

I persisted, explaining that ours would be a softer, tamer Carmen. In addition, we would introduce a character in the tradition of the Opéra-Comique – a young, innocent girl, very pure. True, we would have Gypsies, but Gypsy comedians. And the death of Carmen would be glossed over at the very end, in a holiday atmosphere, with a parade, a ballet, a joyful fanfare. After a long, difficult struggle, M. de Leuven acceded. "But I pray you," he said, "try not to have her die. Death – at the Opéra-Comique! This has never been seen, never! Don't make her die, my young friend, I pray you!" (p. 36)

Whether we take Halévy's report to be accurate or self-serving, earnest or ironic, it does point up the normal expectations at the Opéra-Comique, the ways *Carmen* violated them and the librettists' attempts at appeasing the usual audience. Carmen herself was to be tempered, and the character of Micaëla was offered as a foil. The gypsies were to be rendered innocuous through comedic treatment, and the impact of the death itself was to be blunted by its occurrence within a brilliant, distracting *divertissement*. Despite Halévy's assurances, de Leuven's fears continued unabated – and, indeed, Halévy's insistence that Carmen would be "softer, tamer" and that her death would be "glossed over" seems a bit disingenuous. Still, the project went forward.

Translating a text as convoluted as Mérimée's on to the stage was no easy task, and a few critics have complained that Bizet and his librettists betrayed the novella. Indeed, if one locates Mérimée's ingenuity in *Carmen* in its structural and narratological virtuosity rather than in Don José's lurid story *per se*, then the opera's linear unfolding may seem rather pedestrian. The most drastic alteration in the adaptation of the novella for purposes of opera involves the elimination of the narrator – the omniscient voice that guides us through the story, interpreting what we are permitted to see and hear. Nor is José's narrative voice present in the opera: his is simply one of several competing for attention in what appears to be an unmediated presentation of the events themselves. In other words, we move from the monologic conventions of fiction to the polyvocal conventions of drama.

This attenuation of narrative control was potentially quite perilous. In Mérimée's story, the figure of Carmen was always multiply mediated: through José's recollections, the narrator, Mérimée's language. Yet she had been regarded nonetheless as lethal. Not even José's knife suffices to contain her, and the narrator lunges to erect a moralizing scholarly text to prevent further contagion. In casting aside Mérimée's complex framing devices, the librettists risked creating a simplistic reduction of the novella. But they also risked unleashing a monster even more dangerous than his, for their Carmen would seem to speak for herself without the constant intervention of narrative voices. Given the sensitive nature of the subject matter of this story, this was a problem the collaborators could scarcely afford to overlook. But their strategies of containment had to be radically different from Mérimée's, given the nature of their medium.

The most obvious counterweight added in the opera is Micaëla – a girl from José's home who has been sent to him as a messenger and potential bride by his mother. Mérimée had no such figure: his is a world in which desperate men circle warily around Carmen as though she were the only woman on earth and compete to the death for her favors. However, the dramatic stage – especially the family-oriented stage of the Opéra-Comique – was regarded as a more influential site of social formation than the novel. Because the life-like representations enacted there were more likely to be perceived by impressionable viewers as real than the creatures of fiction, the guidelines surrounding theatrical works were much stricter. Micaëla was designed to contrast with Carmen, as the normative good girl who stands as the ideal against which Carmen herself appears all the more monstrous.

The collaborators also reshaped the lead characters. In the novella, we first meet Don José as a bandit and murderer; only gradually are we brought to see him as a victim. By contrast, the opera introduces him as a relatively innocent soldier, and we witness his downfall at first hand. To be sure, some of Mérimée's prose reappears in the first scenes of the *opéra-comique* version, as José explains briefly how a former act of violence resulted in his being sent to the military for discipline. But his sentimental scene with Micaëla establishes him as a mama's boy; it is almost impossible to identify this persona with the one Mérimée described as resembling Milton's Satan. If the struggle between aggressive Carmen and passive José seems an unequal match in the novella, the odds against him appear overwhelming in the opera.

Halévy promised a "softer, tamer" Carmen, and in certain respects, the opera's Carmen might be seen as laundered. Her criminal activities – for instance, theft – are downplayed. And she no longer functions as leader of the smugglers, but modestly obeys the authority of El Dancaïro: in this sense, at least, she has been domesticated. But Mérimée's Carmen was also a healer who risked her own well-being to save others, and her intelligence is revealed in her direct conversational style. The figure who emerges in the opera operates almost exclusively as a *femme fatale*; her sexuality, which is prominent enough in the novella, constitutes virtually her entire character for the first two acts.

The action is also compressed considerably for the purposes of the opera. While José's narration rambles through several episodes of increasing humiliation, the librettists took only the highlights and arranged them so that they appear to operate according to rapid-fire cause-and-effect. The events of the second act, for example, take place in Mérimée over the course of many months, during which time José is warned repeatedly to leave. In the opera, José's entry begins a sequence that unfolds without pause through his seduction, his attack on Zuniga and his necessary escape with the gypsies. If this streamlining of the novella eliminates much of its ambiguity, it also intensifies the plot's goal-oriented trajectory, causing its conclusion to seem inevitable. The libretto of *Carmen* is justly regarded as one of the most effective, most brilliant in all of opera.

But the most intricate restructuring of the novella for purposes of this opera – the delineation of relative points of view – is principally the work of Bizet, for it takes place within the music itself. It is he who creates vivid images of the Other – Carmen's sexuality, her indicators of racial and class difference – as well as José's utterances. But he locates all of these within a delicate web of musical forms, cultural associations, motivic correspondences and subtle affective commentaries that match or surpass in complexity Mérimée's framing devices, even though they operate on the basis of entirely different premises: the premises of musical procedure. These are examined in detail in Chapter 5.

Bizet did not devote the years between the Opéra-Comique commission in 1872 and the premiere in March 1875 exclusively to *Carmen*. He had believed that rehearsals for *Carmen* would begin in the autumn of 1873, and he wrote the first act with that date in mind. But when the Opéra-Comique postponed production, he turned to other projects. He contributed incidental music for a *mélodrame* by Alphonse Daudet, *L'Arlésienne* (1872), a box-office disaster from which Bizet extracted his music and developed his well-known suite. During 1873 he worked on but never completed *Don Rodrigue*, an opera planned for the Opéra on the subject of El Cid (featuring Spain and a Don José-like Cid whom Bizet characterized as "lover, son, Christian"). He also composed *Patrie*, an overture performed to excellent reviews in 1874, and he was planning an oratorio on the subject of *Geneviève de Paris*. When friends responded coolly to his *Don Rodrigue* sketches, he began to doubt his abilities to write for the stage. But he finally pulled out of his depression and returned to the *Carmen* project. He completed the opera in 1874 and orchestrated it during that summer. Music rehearsals began at last on October 2.

His promised transformation of the *opéra-comique* genre did not proceed smoothly. Early drafts of *Carmen* revealed that the elements of Mérimée's novella over which the Opéra-Comique administration had been apprehensive remained intact in the emerging opera, and de Leuven resigned from his post as co-director early in 1874, in part as a result of the controversy over this opera. Nor was de Leuven alone in doubting *Carmen*'s viability. At various moments in the process, each of Bizet's collaborators urged him to compromise. Meilhac too resisted killing Carmen off, and both he and Halévy tried (to little avail) to tone down the lead performers during rehearsals. In keeping with the performance practices of *opéra-comique*, the librettists also wanted a break for applause after Don José's "Flower Song," which would have destroyed the dramatic impact of Carmen's pianissimo response, "Non, tu ne m'aimes pas." Here and elsewhere, Bizet refused to yield. Late into the rehearsal schedule, Du Locle tried to demand that the ending be changed, and he even called in an outside arbitrator. When the lead singers threatened to quit over this issue, however, he backed down. But he broadcast his opinion that the music Bizet had written was "Cochin-Chinese and utterly incomprehensible,"[7] and he is thought to have published the disclaimer that appeared in newspapers on the day of the premiere. Moreover, just before the opening, Halévy attempted to distance himself from the project (see the quotation above). According to a witness:

For the only time in his life, during the rehearsals of *Carmen*, Ludovic Halévy, that wisest, most balanced, most philosophical of men, lost his composure. But he felt what we all did, and Bizet more than any of us, that for the composer this was the decisive test, the turning point in his career. His emotion was as profound as his hopes were high. The slightest shock set him to vibrating like a taut wire. The theatre gossip that seeped through the half-open door of the director's office and whistled through the wings and the dressing-rooms like a threatening wind before a storm, shook his confidence for the first time.[8]

Bizet also had to contend with resistance from performers. The part of Carmen proved difficult to cast. When Zulma Bouffar (a singer associated with Offenbach) refused the role, a gossip columnist explained that "Meilhac did *not* wish her to play the part because it was out of the question for Zulma to be stabbed."[9] A second choice, Marie Roze, turned it down after meeting with Bizet. She wrote to him:

The tragic end of *Carmen* had made me presuppose dramatic action that would modify the very scabrous side of this character; the explanations you were kind enough to make to me at the outset of our interview having showed me that the character was to be scrupulously respected, I understood immediately that the role would not suit me, or, more accurately, that I would not be suited to it.[10]

Finally, Galli-Marié (who confessed to never having heard of Mérimée's *Carmen*) accepted the part, and she became Bizet's staunchest ally in the production. She brought to the role fine musicianship, powerful acting abilities and a high degree of professionalism. She resisted the librettists' attempts at taming Bizet's vision of Carmen, and she even collaborated with him in the composition of the "Habañera." She also persuaded Paul Lhérie to play the part of Don José. Galli-Marié and Lhérie eventually preserved the integrity of the original narrative by blocking Du Locle's attempts at changing the ending.

But problems arose from other members of the company. The chorus, which ordinarily performed in oratorio fashion – that is, motionless and facing the conductor – rebelled against what it regarded as the impossible task of singing while moving. According to Halévy:

Most of the singers were bewildered and threatened to strike. After two months of rehearsal, they insisted that the two first-act choruses were unperformable: the entrance of the cigarette girls and the scuffle around the officer after the arrest of Carmen. These two choruses, very difficult to play . . . necessitated not only singing, but at the same time motion, action, coming and going – life, in short. This was without precedent at the Opéra-Comique. The members of the chorus were in the habit of singing the ensembles, standing motionless in line, their arms slack, their eyes fixed on the conductor's baton, their thoughts elsewhere.[11]

Bizet refused to change his concept, but requested instead that ten more women be hired for the chorus. He wrote du Locle in mid-January:

As you are making great sacrifices for *Carmen*, please allow me to do one small thing to assure the proper execution of my women's choruses in the first act. Meilhac and Halévy want faces, and I would like some voices! Authorize me to take six additional first-upper-voices and four second-upper-voices ... The women are there. I will rehearse them myself tomorrow, *Sunday*, and the *day after, Monday!* They can take their places on stage *Tuesday*. I shall do *everything necessary* so that the choruses will be ready in three days. Please forgive my frenzy, but don't think that I am selfish; if I were alone before the enemy, I should be less disturbed. But you are with me; you are risking more than I am. I sense a possible victory, I assure you, and I know that you will be repaid by it. It's a matter of honor, and also, *cher ami*, of feeling (original emphasis).[12]

Only after Halévy investigated the situation and reported back that these singers were necessary did Du Locle reluctantly agree to the additional expense. Halévy later testified that the orchestra also agitated against what were perceived as unplayable sections in the score, but that after extensive extra rehearsals they managed to perform adequately. In addition, during the rehearsal period (October 2, 1874 through March 3, 1875), sessions for *Carmen* had to compete for space and time with the more than twenty other productions in repertory at the Opéra-Comique. Fully staged rehearsals with scenery became possible only in the two weeks preceding opening night. The set designs for the first production of *Carmen* have only recently been located and identified by Evan Baker.[13]

The rest of our information concerning rehearsals must be gleaned indirectly from surviving scores and libretti. Comparisons between the original conducting score and the score sold to Choudens for publication two months before the premiere indicate that Bizet made many substantial changes during the course of the rehearsal period itself. Scholars differ in their interpretations of the various versions. On the one hand, Fritz Oeser, who rediscovered the conducting score and used it as the basis for a critical edition, maintains that this version records Bizet's intentions, which were subverted during production.[14] But on the other hand, Winton Dean and Lesley Wright contend that the Choudens score represents Bizet's own revisions, arrived at through benefit of rehearsals. They argue compellingly that virtually all the changes serve to focus, streamline and refine his earlier formulations and that Oeser's edition therefore inadvertently preserves as definitive an early draft of the opera.[15]

In fact, none of the changes responds to the objections raised by either collaborators or performers: the difficult sections remain, the exotic sensuality of the gypsies pervades the score, and Don José's murder of Carmen reigns unblunted as the horrific climax of the opera. Dean and, subsequently, Wright have documented in detail the modifications introduced into the score before the premiere. The *mélodrame* sections were more extensive in the first score, but many of them were eliminated during rehearsals. A reminiscence motive based on Carmen's fatalistic section of the Card Scene originally appeared twice – in the finale to Act III and at the end, just after Don José has stabbed her. The finales to Acts I, III and IV were revised several times over to maximize dramatic intensity.

Moreover, Bizet occasionally rethought not only his music, but also the libretto. Galli-Marié rejected the first version of the "Habañera" as an unacceptable vehicle for her initial entrance. Bizet had set Halévy's original verses, which were excessively wordy, in an equally uninspired manner. According to Galli-Marié's testimony, they went through thirteen drafts together before they arrived at the final version. They settled on a popular cabaret tune by the Spanish-Cuban composer Sebastián Yradier (see Chapter 4) and then sent Halévy a schematic outline (a "monstre") that indicated the verse forms, lines and syllables needed. Halévy presented another set of lines, which were then reworked by Bizet and, presumably, Galli-Marié.

While rehearsals for *Carmen* proceeded, Bizet took time to attend César Franck's organ course at the Conservatoire, perhaps because of his interest in writing an oratorio. The day before the premiere, he appeared in Franck's class with complimentary tickets. He is reported to have said: "But there are eight of you and I have only two tickets. Unfortunately that is too few; but you know even the most beautiful girl in the world can give no more than she has."[16] D'Indy was one of the recipients of the tickets, and he later assisted in performances of *Carmen* by playing the harmonium while Lhérie sang his unaccompanied march in Act II – Lhérie was merely the first of many Don Josés who find it difficult to stay on pitch during that number.

The premiere of *Carmen* occurred on March 3, 1875. On the

morning of that day, it was announced that Bizet had been nominated to the Legion of Honor, an irony that echoes a similar event in Mérimée's career: Mérimée too had created an uproar when, on the day after his election to the Académie française in 1844, his novella *Arsène Guillot* appeared in the *Revue des deux mondes*. The audience assembled for *Carmen*'s first performance differed considerably from the usual Opéra-Comique crowd. Du Locle had warned some potential audience members to stay away from the opera, afraid that they would be so offended by what they saw that the Opéra-Comique's reputation would be irredeemably jeopardized. But the music community (composers such as Gounod, Massenet, d'Indy, Delibes, Offenbach, as well as prominent performers and music publishers) attended in full force. Idlers who sensed the possibility of a scandal also showed up to be entertained. If this audience was scandalized, it was scarcely because it was composed of bourgeois families. Halévy later recounted *Carmen*'s opening night reception:

The entry of Carmen was well received and applauded, as was the duet between Micaela and Don José. As the first act ended there were many curtain calls. Backstage, Bizet was surrounded, congratulated!

The second act, less enthusiasm. It opened brilliantly. The entrance of Escamillo was most effective. But then the audience cooled . . . surprised, unhappy, ill-at-ease. Backstage, fewer admirers, congratulations restrained. No enthusiasm at all for the third act except for Micaela's aria. The audience was frigid during the fourth act. Only a few devotees of Bizet came backstage. *Carmen* was not a success. Meilhac and I walked home with Bizet. Our hearts were heavy.[17]

As everyone knows, the first production of *Carmen* was received very badly. A few of Bizet's musical colleagues expressed appreciation for what he had accomplished. Massenet, for instance, wrote: "How happy you must be at this time! – *It's a great success*. When I have the good fortune to see you, I shall tell you how happy you made me . . . Again bravo with all my heart"; and Saint-Saëns wrote: "At last I have seen *Carmen*. I found it marvelous and I am telling you the truth."[18] But others, such as Gounod (formerly one of Bizet's protectors), gloated over the apparent failure of the opera. One of Gounod's younger students witnessed his duplicity and recorded how during intermission he flattered Bizet lavishly to his face, but how, after he returned to the audience, he revealed his actual reactions:

Micaëla sang her now well-known air, which the public encored. Gounod leaned forward in his box and applauded enthusiastically so that all could see. Then he took his seat again and sighed: "That melody is mine! Georges has robbed me; take the Spanish airs and mine out of the score, and there remains nothing to Bizet's credit but the sauce that masks the fish."[19]

Several reviews appeared in the newspapers in the days that followed. With the exception of one by Théodore de Banville, they were almost uniformly devastating. These, along with subsequent moments of *Carmen* reception, are examined in Chapter 6. The initial production of *Carmen* ran for forty-eight performances to small audiences. Du Locle considered cutting the run short for financial reasons, but was persuaded – again by Galli-Marié and perhaps Bizet's publisher, Choudens – to allow it to complete the original schedule of performances.

In the meantime, Bizet's health began to fail. Always chronically ill, especially in periods of emotional stress, Bizet seems to have succumbed once again to throat abscesses and muscular rheumatism. He departed in late May for his home in the country to convalesce, and he appeared to improve considerably – enough to go swimming in the Seine. A few days later, however, he was struck with a high fever and then a heart attack. A second heart attack early in the morning of June 3 killed him. It was three months after *Carmen*'s disastrous opening and just after its thirty-third performance. The production closed at the Opéra-Comique on February 15, 1876. But by that time, *Carmen* had conquered Vienna and was on its way to glory.

3 Images of race, class and gender in nineteenth-century French culture

Bizet's *Carmen* has often been understood as a story of ill-fated love between two equal parties whose destinies happen to clash. But to read the opera in this fashion is to ignore the faultlines of social power that organize it, for while the story's subject matter may appear idiosyncratic to us, *Carmen* is actually only one of a large number of fantasies involving race, class and gender that circulated in nineteenth-century French culture. Thus before exploring the opera on its own terms, we need to reexamine the critical tensions of its original context – the context within which it was written and first received – as well as the politics of representation: who creates representations of whom, with what imagery, towards what ends?

Musicologists have long recognized *Carmen*'s exoticism as one of its most salient features, but they usually treat that exoticism as unproblematic. Indeed, until quite recently, most of the exotic images and narratives that proliferate in Western culture were regarded as innocent: the "Orient" (first the Middle East, later East Asia and Africa) seemed to serve merely as a "free zone" for the European imagination. Edward Said, however, has shown that this "free zone" was always circumscribed by political concerns.[1] Some of these were relatively benign. In the eighteenth century, for instance, the "Orient" offered a vantage point from which French writers could criticize their own society. Thus Rousseau addressed the East as a utopian philosopher contemplating alternatives with the West, and Montesquieu adopted the persona of a Persian traveler writing letters home about the odd social practices he encounters in Paris.[2]

But serious "Orientalism" dates from Napoleon's Egyptian campaign of 1798, an invasion that stimulated the growth of academic disciplines investigating Middle Eastern archaeology, religions, linguistics and anthropology. While many Orientalist scholars no doubt believed they were amassing disinterested knowledge, their information was also mobilized for purposes of state and commercial colonization. As Christopher Miller writes, "Orientalism must be seen from a dual perspective. For participants in the movement, the Orient was an intellectual adventure based on realistic acts of *description*; from a late 20th-century point of view, 'orientalism' is a political mythology passing itself off as objective truth."[3]

French artists soon began to manifest a profound fascination with things Middle Eastern. Victor Hugo defined the terrain and agenda of cultural "Orientalism" succinctly in the preface to his collection of poetry *Les Orientales* (1829):

The Orient, as image or as thought, has become, for the intelligence as well as for the imagination, a sort of general preoccupation which the author of this book has obeyed perhaps without his knowledge. Oriental colors came as of their own accord to imprint themselves on all his thoughts, all his dreams; and his dreams and his thoughts found themselves in turn, and almost without having wished it so, Hebraic, Turkish, Greek, Persian, Arab, even Spanish, because Spain is still the Orient; Spain is half African, Africa is half Asiatic.[4]

Several details in this manifesto are worthy of note. First, Hugo describes (surely somewhat disingenuously) his exploitation of the East not as active volition, but rather as the East's having seduced him into surrendering his Western rationality over to its agendas. He presents himself as a prototype of Don José, lured by the mystery and sensual overload of the "Orient" into deserting the Apollonian poetic tradition of the *ancien régime*: in Hugo's words, "In the age of Louis XIV one was a Hellenist; now one is an Orientalist." The statement above also indicates without apology the radical interchangeability of exotic types for the cultural Orientalist: Persian, Greek, Jewish, Spanish, African – all wash together in an undifferentiated realm of Otherness.

Hugo's discussion of Spain is especially important for our purposes. Whatever the reality of Spain's history or culture, French Orientalists ascribed to it the same inscrutable, luxuriant and barbarous qualities they imagined to be characteristic of the entire Middle East. In his preface, Hugo writes rapturously about Spain, especially the tension – described with lavishly gender-coded language – between the austerity of its gothic Christian remnants and the mystery of its Moorish elements "opened out to the sun like a large flower full of perfumes."

Within his imagined, autonomous realm of "the Orient," Hugo can safely construct his poems of bloodthirsty warriors, pirates, djinn, harem girls. Central to his many verses on exotic women is the veil: that sign of ownership, modesty and intrigue which can be coaxed into lifting for the pleasure of poet and reader alike.[5] While such images of denuded harem girls may seem innocuous enough, in fact they participated in a much larger socio-cultural agenda. In Orientalist texts these women stand for the East itself: veiled in mystery but finally penetrable by the Western desire to know and possess. The East as a whole became "feminized," understood as sensual, static, irrational and nonproductive, though fertile with resources and ripe for plunder. The East's seductiveness seemed even to invite its own ravishment, just as Hugo claims he enters this terrain "perhaps without his knowledge" – and just as Don José, Mérimée's narrator and we, the audience are lured into Carmen's world "almost without having wished it."

Unfortunately, these tropes informed and reinforced the pillaging and conquest of the Middle East during this same period. As Said explains, French officials drew upon the vivid fictions of novelists and painters in shaping their Middle Eastern policies. The consequences of cultural Orientalism have been played out on the bodies of real people whose lives have very little to do with the fantasies concocted by European artists. The disastrous political condition of the Middle East today is among the legacies of exoticism and its colorful representations.

Political imperialism was not, of course, Hugo's motive for *Les Orientales*. Hugo turned to the East because of its "fecundity," its sensuality, its license, its cruelty – and also because in his fantasized Orient, he was able to experience the plenitude he felt to be lacking in urban France. For if the European imagination found itself drawn irresistibly towards the exotic, it was in part because of a growing belief that Western culture was bankrupt. The "Orient" thus became a kind of utopian projection, a place offering in unchecked profusion those qualities the West had traditionally denied itself through Christian prohibition, political oppression or regimented bourgeois mores. Repressed desires and grievances emerged and found an outlet for expression, however displaced, in Orientalism. As in the eighteenth century, Orientalist culture still contained within it a component of cultural critique that permitted artists and the public to imagine other, perhaps more liberated, forms of social life.

But if part of the motivation for Orientalism was to criticize the West and its attitudes towards Others (Hugo writes that "ancient Asiatic barbarism was perhaps not so devoid of superior men as our civilization wishes to believe"), that very critique constituted a threat to the belief in Western supremacy that underwrote the colonizing enterprise. The idealization of the East easily and frequently led to a backlash of reimposed Western domination, especially in narratives in which the Westerner surrenders all claims to privilege and "goes primitive," but then tries to reverse the process, reasserting domination all the more insistently for having let it slip. As Marianne Torgovnick puts it, "the West's fascination with the primitive has to do with its own crises in identity, with its own need to clearly demarcate subject and object even while flirting with other ways of experiencing the universe."[6]

The tension between desire for the exotic and fear of its seductive potency runs through many of the cultural artifacts of Orientalism – including *Carmen*, which was written at a time when France was experiencing particular humiliation with respect to its position as a world power. Nelly Furman writes, "after the 'ignominious' defeat of the French army in the Franco-Prussian War of 1870, during which the Emperor Napoleon III and his armed forces were taken prisoner at Sedan, Bizet's opera shows us a well-meaning but naive soldier beguiled by an enticing foreigner. Napoleon III had married a Spaniard ... By implying that the woman causes the soldier's downfall, as traditional interpretations of the opera suggest, Bizet and the librettists ... seem to propose a psychological explanation for a political and military event."[7]

Hugo's *Les Orientales* was followed by an outpouring of Orientalist novels, poems and paintings. Unlike many of his colleagues who fabricated images of the "Orient" without setting foot outside France, Flaubert actually toured the Middle East, gathering materials that stimulated his creative imagination. Predictably, he focused on transgressive sexual practices, which he sampled systematically and wrote home about *ad nauseam*. *Salammbô* is but one of the Orientalist fantasies he wrote upon his return to France. Ingres' languorous nudes lounging in seraglios are the most famous such images in the visual arts.

Music too participated throughout the history of Orientalism. From the seventeenth century on, operas had regularly made use of exotic settings, although the music itself only occasionally was designed to sound "Oriental." Nineteenth-century musical Orientalism began soon after the Egyptian Expedition and became enthusiastically Arabic around 1830 – just after the French conquest of Algiers.[8] The themes that mark literary and artistic Orientalism show up in music as well. Félicien David, for instance, visited the Middle East, and his music reflects both his impressions and French cultural concerns. His *Le Désert* (1844) depicts caravans, muezzins calling the faithful to prayer and the ubiquitous dancing girls.

During the second half of the century, Orientalism saturated opera production in France. In the discussion of "exoticism" in his *Nineteenth-Century Music*, Carl Dahlhaus explains this trend by reproducing uncritically the attitude that ethnic cultures merely provided raw materials to stimulate the exhausted European imagination. He writes, "exoticism offered nineteenth-century opera librettists an *untapped reservoir of material that virtually cried out for exploitation*" (emphasis added).[9] Some of the operas that resulted from this supposedly solicited exploitation include Gounod's *La Reine de Saba* (1862), Saint-Saëns' *Samson et Dalila* (1877), Delibes' *Lakmé* (1883) and Massenet's *Thaïs* (1894). Even instrumental music indulged in this fashion, as in d'Indy's *Istar* (1912), a set of variations that begins with the most extravagant version and casts off veil after veil until the theme itself – identified as the goddess Istar – is revealed gloriously naked.

Bizet's infatuation with exoticism can be traced as far back as his Symphony in C, a piece completed when he was seventeen, which features Orientalist themes in its inner movements. Such subjects persisted throughout his career. *Djamileh* is a full-fledged Orientalist fantasy, involving a slave girl who begs her master to reenslave her (the dénouement involves her unveiling). Some of his other exotic moments required some connivance: *La Jolie Fille de Perth* is set in Scotland, but features a band of gypsies who suddenly materialize for a ballet; *Carmen* engages with Hugo's Orientalist Spain. The music Bizet wrote to represent the exotic rarely had much to do ethnographically with the purported locales of these operas, but he knew how to invoke with uncanny deftness the French notion of the racial Other (see Chapter 4).

Carmen differs from many Orientalist texts in that its terrain is not uniformly exotic. The opera involves an encounter between an aristocrat of northern stock, marked as "one of us," and a gypsy, who bears most of the burden of exoticism for the duration of the composition. Thus *Carmen* operates in part as an Orientalist work, but it also participates in another genre prevalent in nineteenth-century France: that of the racial Other who has infiltrated home turf.

For not all "Orientals" were located in imaginary lands. Two principal groups classified as Oriental – gypsies and Jews – circulated in French society.[10] While occupying very different positions within that society, they were often presented in cultural artifacts (which exploited them in part for exotic color) as interchangeable. Thus the gypsy Esmeralda in Hugo's *Notre Dame de Paris* is first taken to be Jewish, as is Mérimée's Carmen. Balzac identifies Esther, the martyred prostitute in his *Splendors and Miseries of a Courtesan*, as a Jew and describes her as Oriental, mysterious, pagan, sexually precocious.

Far more than actual Middle Easterners, gypsies and Jews were regarded as dangerous, for while marked as alien, they lived on native soil. They were too real; they passed through the boundaries between European Self and Other that made classic Orientalism safe for the aesthetic gaze. And both groups were linguistically treacherous: they mastered the languages of their host countries so as to be able to "pass" as indigenous, while retaining fluency in their own archaic tongues – tongues that remained opaque to those around them. Carmen's linguistic versatility is one of her greatest threats in Mérimée, and Bizet constructs her with a similar virtuosity with respect to musical discourses (see Chapters 1 and 4).

The boundaries of race or ethnicity were not the only ones threatened by these groups: issues of class and sexuality were inextricably bound up with popular perceptions of the "Orientals" at home. The label "bohemian," for instance, could refer to the gypsies or to the underclass subculture that became a breeding ground for both avant-garde artists and political unrest.[11] Gypsies performed their exotic songs and dances for the benefit of popular audiences in Paris, and Bizet (along with his collaborator for *L'Arlésienne*, Alphonse Daudet) frequented their haunts of ill-repute for entertainment. "Local color" was available, in other words, as a constant feature of Parisian night-life: the "Orient" had been reconstituted at home, and one could dabble in exotic women and music without ever leaving the city.

Jews would seem to have little in common with migrant gypsies. By the nineteenth century, they had become leaders in France in the arts, the economy and politics. Yet the status of artists such as Meyerbeer or the Halévys did not prevent Jews from being regarded as foreign parasites. The Dreyfus Affair later revealed the virulence of French anti-Semitism, but novels by Balzac and the Goncourts had already depicted Jews as sinister, sexually depraved outsiders. Hitler's genocidal agenda (in which many of the French participated) grouped Jews with gypsies and "sexual deviants" as targets for extermination. *Carmen* becomes far more complicated when lifted from Hugo's "Orient" and resituated within a domestic context that was experiencing tensions between the "pure-blooded" European and the dark, seductive interloper.

Contemporary tensions bound up with class likewise pervade *Carmen*. In the years since the French Revolution, the dominant middle class in France had advanced through several phases. Initially, universal emancipation was embraced as the proper liberal sentiment. But as the working class began pushing for its own liberation, the contradictions undergirding the French bourgeoisie became increasingly apparent. Since middle-class living standards required a large, malleable labor force, the bourgeoisie was reluctant to extend parity to workers. Revolutions rocked France in 1830, 1848 and 1871, causing many middle-class individuals to perceive the disenfranchised as alien (if necessary) presences. Demands for rights were received as violent threats, the sordid poverty of the underclass seen as a cesspool breeding crime and promiscuity. Bizet introduces Carmen as a common laborer in a cigar factory patroled by Don José's military unit. During Act I, we witness the violence of this working class in Carmen's knife fight with her co-worker, her insubordination with Zuniga, her treachery with José. Later we are treated to scenes of smuggling and prostitution. None of this would have seemed coincidental in 1875, a scant four years after the trauma of the Commune.

Despite its general loathing of the proletariat, some members of the middle class, especially those inclined to be artists, aligned themselves with the underclass through the bohemian subculture. Without question, these dropouts greatly romanticized the conditions of working-class life; yet the factors that drew them to abandon their middle-class comforts resembled those that caused the "Orient" to appear so attractive at this same time: release from a regimented bureaucratic society and rigid sexual mores that demanded the sacrifice of pleasure for duty.[12] Carmen appeals to Don José in part because she offers him freedom from the strictures of his bourgeois life. But the cost of his escape from respectability soon becomes clear. His descent into the underworld is dramatically

conveyed through his abdication of the bright public street of Act I
for the den of iniquity of Act II and the uninhabited wilderness of
Act III. He reemerges into the light of Act IV as a dissolute,
common criminal wandering the streets.

Interestingly, Bizet himself was branded a "bohemian" by his
in-laws, the Halévy family, who initially resisted his marriage
proposal on those grounds. To be sure, Bizet's bohemianism
remained rather shallow: it seems to have been limited to his
promiscuity and penchant for night-time slumming. It did not affect
his political attitudes, for he – like many affluent bourgeois – fled
Paris in disgust during the Commune. Yet both Bizet's flirtation
with the underclass and his subsequent recoiling from it might be
considered possible factors in his compulsion to set Mérimée's
Carmen.

But an even more important factor in the appeal of *Carmen* was
Mérimée's treatment of sexuality, which engaged so effectively
nineteenth-century cultural ambivalences concerning women. As
with issues of race and class, the earlier nineteenth century had
dealt with women through narratives of benign co-existence, possible so long as an unchallenged hierarchy prevailed. Just as the
"Orient" seemed to serve as the passive landscape upon which the
Western artist projected his fantasies and the working class
appeared to labor voluntarily under the conditions of capitalist
industry, so women were thought to thrive in domestic confine-
ment, their energies absorbed by the duties of wife and mother.
The assumed dominance of the white, middle-class male guaranteed that all these relationships – whether of race, class or gender –
appeared to reflect the natural order of things.

In literature and painting of the mid-century, chaste, domestic
female figures abound. This stereotype found one of its most
striking realizations in Coventry Patmore's *The Angel in the House*
(1863), in which the sexless, selfless wife and mother maintains the
spiritual and material comforts of the hearth as compensation for
the depersonalized public workplace.[13] On the French stage, her
most reliable venue was the Opéra-Comique, which had exalted
this figure in operas for several decades; she was one of the defining
characteristics of the *opéra-comique* genre and appeared as heroine
in Auber, Gounod and in *La Dame blanche*, the opera so detested
by Bizet. She resurfaced as Micaëla in *Carmen*, and she even
entered Bizet's life in the form of Geneviève Halévy. In 1867 the
notorious womanizer reported his infatuation with his wife-to-be

thus: "No more *soirées*! No more sprees! No more mistresses! All that is finished! Absolutely finished! I am saying this seriously. I have met an adorable girl whom I love! In two years she will be my wife! ... I tell you this seriously; I am convinced! I am sure of myself! The good has killed the evil! The victory is won!"[14]

The majority of middle-class women in the nineteenth century complied with hegemonic ideals of femininity: they withdrew from participation in the public sphere, and some even denied themselves sexual expression in conformity with the images proliferating in conduct manuals, novels and operas. But many women rejected the prescribed role of "angel in the house." As Peter Gay writes, "Man's fear of woman is as old as time, but it was only in the bourgeois century that it became a prominent theme in popular novels and medical treatises ... Men's defensiveness in the bourgeois century was so acute because the advance of women all around them was an attempt to recover ground they had lost."[15]

Accordingly, the images in culture began to shift, from reveries of benevolent submission within a preordained hierarchy to nightmares involving powerfully constituted, monstrous Others threatening to overwhelm the weakened, victimized dominant order. Sexually assertive, self-willed women appeared increasingly in novels and paintings in the last decades of the century. According to Gay, "Woman as vampire, man as victim: that was, if not the general consensus, a strong current of male feeling in nineteenth-century France."[16] Eventually, the *femme fatale* shows up in opera as well – with a vengeance. Bizet himself describes Myrrha, the Carmen-like *femme fatale* in his *La Coupe du Roi de Thulé*, in these words:

She is an old-style courtesan, sensual as Sappho, ambitious as Aspasia; she is beautiful, quick-witted, alluring ... In her eyes must be that greenish look, the sure sign of sensuality and egoism pushed to the length of cruelty ... Yorick by himself is free; he sings his love with passion and frenzy; he tells it to the clouds and the stars. With Myrrha present he is extinguished ... She comes in (for the first time) slowly, dreamily, absent-mindedly; she turns her glance on all around her, and fixes it almost disdainfully on Yorick.[17]

To be sure, feminine sexuality had not been absent from culture during the earlier part of the century. Cultural portraits of the "Oriental," the Jew, the gypsy or the working class often foregrounded gender, substituting "Woman" metonymically for the Middle East, the alien at home or the exploited poor. Motivations for all of these are curiously similar: the thwarted desires of middle-class males sought expression in each of these fantasy lands, and they often enacted their release on the imagined or actual bodies of women. But because such men wanted to preserve the purity of their own homes, the preferred objects of taboo practices were racial or underclass Others – women viewed as available, uninhibited and wanton by nature. That Bizet shared this weakness for "exotic" women is clear from his letters detailing his sexual adventures in Italy during his Prix de Rome.

During the nineteenth century, prostitution thrived in Paris as never before, in part because economic conditions made this the only means of survival for hundreds of homeless, poverty-stricken women.[18] But prostitution could not have flourished as it did without the patronage of men from all levels of society, including the artistic and social elite. Much of the high art from this period – major works and personal letters by Balzac, Baudelaire, Zola, Courbet, Manet – exploits prostitution as a central theme. Moreover, the art world itself was saturated with prostitution: women who modeled, danced or sang in public were assumed to be and were treated as whores. The costume balls at the Opéra allowed patrons to arrange liaisons with performers; Ludovic Halévy wrote a salacious novel (illustrations by Degas) on *bons vivants* trafficking in showgirls;[19] and Meilhac too was a noted connoisseur of such women.

Bizet's well-documented exploitation of prostitutes has already been mentioned, but one figure in his life in the *demi-monde* deserves special treatment. In 1865 he met a woman who lived near his father's country home. Comtesse Lionel de Chabrillan was born Céleste Vénard, an illegitimate child who fled her abusive family at thirteen. She became a *fille inscrite* – a prostitute registered with the Paris police. By sixteen, she was involved with the poet Alfred de Musset and soon left the brothels to appear as a dancer at the Bal Mabille where she was named "La Mogador," after a Moroccan city recently bombarded by the French. She became a celebrity who traveled in the same circles as prominent figures in French culture. After marrying the Comte de Chabrillan, she was at last removed from the police register. She then turned to writing, and although she had no formal education and notated her works phonetically, she became a prolific and popular author of novels, libretti, plays and memoirs.[20] When Bizet met her, she was a forty-one-year-old widow, writing but still singing at the popular Café-Concert du

XIXième Siècle. Since her repertory included songs by Yradier, it is possible she introduced Bizet to the song that became the "Habañera." In any case, she took Bizet under her protection, permitted him to use her house as a retreat in which to compose, and even bought him a piano.

Unlike most such women, Céleste found the means of accounting for her own life in her writing – of representing herself. Her candid views of Bizet (who may or may not have been her lover) describe him as "an aristocratic savage": "I never saw him laugh outright. Georges Bizet was not very gay at this time. He was still living on hope."[21] Critics have suggested that Céleste was a model for Carmen, especially because of her vivid self-characterization:

My character was formed early. I loved passionately or hated furiously . . . When I hate people, I wish they would die . . . Moderation is no part of my nature. Joy, sorrow, affection, resentment, laziness, work – I have overdone them all. My life has been one long excess . . . I feel with a passion that devours me . . . When I take up a book, I want to understand it so quickly that the blood rushes to my head. I can't see straight, and I have to stop. Then I go into a ridiculous rage at myself . . . I beat my brain. When I try to learn to write and my hand disobeys, I pinch my arm black and blue . . . Two defects in my character have protected me. I have always been capricious and proud. No one, among women whose tendency it is to say *yes*, derives more pleasure than I do from saying *no*. So the men to whom I have given the most are those who asked least of me.[22]

Carmen clearly belongs to this category of women. She is known to the men in the community as available – albeit (as she makes clear in the "Habañera") on her own terms. She tells Don José in the "Seguidilla" that she often changes lovers and that she frequents Lillas Pastia's, a house of ill-repute in which she and other women provide entertainment, consort with patrons and arrange liaisons for after hours. Her gypsy comrades at Pastia's joke with her about her new-found "love," and José's senior officer tries to set up a routine assignation. Even though Zuniga and Escamillo are put off temporarily, they both assume they are simply awaiting their turns. Bizet's relationship with the benevolent Céleste might account for much of Carmen's strength of character and her positive attributes. But this relationship was not by any means his sole model, for the story of *Carmen* takes some nasty turns – in keeping with the many other treatments of prostitution in French culture of the time.

Prostitution, like "Orientalism" and bohemian slumming, posed severe threats along with its apparent delights, and literary texts of the period explore the various ways in which men feared these women. According to Charles Bernheimer, the prostitute in nineteenth-century French literature

is imagined as animalistic, intense, a sensual feast for the blasé upper-class male. But almost immediately her sexuality becomes threatening. She is somehow impenetrable even as she gives herself to be penetrated, opaque just when she should be most readable. She asserts her independence of the male plot at the very moment when the male thinks he is inscribing her body into it. This assertion, which stimulates narratively productive castration fears, becomes the object of complex strategies designed to put these fears to rest and achieve narrative closure.[23]

Earlier in the century, narratives concerning the prostitute often centered on her moral redemption by a man who is able to see beyond her degraded condition to the essentially kind creature she actually is. In the socially-critical texts of Balzac's *Splendors and Miseries of a Courtesan* and Eugène Sue's *The Mysteries of Paris*, true love rehabilitates the woman who has fallen because of economic destitution, although the indelible taint of her former sin seems to require that she (unlike Céleste Mogador, for instance) sacrifice her life.

Even in these early texts, the woman of color stands as a site of untamed female desire.[24] Balzac's Jewess Esther cannot be cured of lust and nearly dies when forced to practice celibacy in the convent. Sue assigns a devouring, bestial sexuality only to his mulatto prostitute: "a serpent that silently fascinates its prey, sucks it in little by little, enlaces it in inextricable coils, deliberately crushes it, feels it palpitate under its slow bites, and seems to feed as much on its suffering as on its blood."[25] And Baudelaire's "Sed Non Satiata" calls the black woman who dominates her white male lover a "demon without pity." Such descriptions resemble those applied to Carmen in the novella, the opera and subsequent criticism.

Later texts tend to present all prostitutes as embodiments of depraved sexuality, as *femmes fatales* seeking the destruction of men. In Zola's *Nana* or the influential stories of Jules Barbey d'Aurevilly, female desire is described in lurid detail and then violently purged, often in ways that make Don José's thrust of the knife seem quite tame.[26] This change of emphasis is often masked by the stylistic designator "Realism": the moment when the veil of

bourgeois euphemism was stripped away to reveal things –
especially women – "as they really are."[27]

Don José wanders through Bizet's opera as a naïf who has never
learned the cues of his society. The other men – the soldiers, the
gypsies, Escamillo – all read Carmen through the codes of prostitution. Only Don José expects to experience something authentic
in his encounter with her. Throughout the opera, he dreams that he
can redeem her, as Alfredo does Violetta. But Carmen does not
surrender to his romantic plot: she proves incorrigible and returns
back into circulation. Since he can neither possess nor rehabilitate
her, Don José moves to match her "Realist" mode: the strength of
her unrepentant sexuality "forces" him to resort to violence.

Beyond psychological anxieties, nineteenth-century prostitution
raised another, far more lethal danger: venereal disease. Epidem-
ics of syphilis ravaged this world, making "liberating" sexual
encounters potential sites of fatal infection. The dread of female
sexuality that runs through all of Western culture (as far back as
Biblical laws declaring menstruation and childbirth "unclean")
became virulently misogynist during this era. Literary texts lurch in
tormented alternation between a desire to "know" the mysteries of
the unveiled female body and a dread of women's sexuality.
Syphilis represented a true equalizer of men at this time, as the
prostitute transmitted the pollution of underclass depravity to
those seeking to impose their privilege on her body. Baudelaire's
Les Fleurs du mal and Huysmans' *A rebours* bear witness to the
pathology attributed to women's bodies at this time.

Even when disease was absent, this disgust came to be directed at
all women who were sexually active. Only through complete
repression of her sexuality could a woman hope to escape the
weight of these cultural associations, and even at that, there was
always the risk that lifting the veil would reveal the horror of her
female essence. The late nineteenth century waged war on women
in cultural texts that either sanitized them or rendered them as
monstrous, in "scientific" attempts at theorizing femininity by
Darwin or Freud, and in medical establishments that institutional-
ized or mutilated female patients to "free" them of their sexual
impulses.[28]

The character Micaëla in *Carmen* was designed to serve as a foil
to Carmen herself, and her sexlessness pervades her portrayal. Yet
when she first appears on stage, Bizet gives her an accompaniment
that is slippery and chromatic – the musical signs of the classic

femme fatale. The ogling soldiers respond accordingly and must be firmly taught that she is *not*, in fact, just like all the rest. By contrast, Carmen's entrance more than satisfies their expectations through the voluptuous liquidity of her "Habañera." Don José falls victim to her contamination, and by the second act, symptoms of chromatic slippage begin to mark his discourse – as at the end of his "Flower Song." In their final encounter, it is José who is riddled with the results of their contact – it is his chromatic excess and sex-induced madness that lead to the savage conclusion.

An opera in 1875 that presented the color *and* the filth of the "Orient," the insubordination of an indigenous workforce and the lethal contagion of female sexuality faced the risk of arousing public indignation, as Flaubert's *Madame Bovary* or Baudelaire's *Les Fleurs du mal* had twenty years before. And *Carmen* did just that with its first audiences and critics. But by engaging nearly all the controversial themes of late nineteenth-century culture simultaneously, its scandal and eventual success were virtually assured. As we shall see in Chapter 6, *Carmen*'s "realistic" treatment of race, class and gender formed the basis of its initial horrified rejection and also set the terms of its exuberant acceptance the following year.

To be sure, race, ethnicity, class and gender are separate issues, and they must not be confused. We are concerned here, however, with representational constructs, with a story from a moment in European history in which slippage among all varieties of Others informed cultural artifacts. Sander Gilman and Klaus Theweleit have written extensively about the ways in which Jews, gypsies, women, the working classes and the insane were lumped together in the late nineteenth century as a single bloody tide threatening to overwhelm European social order.[29] In 1895, Edouard Drumont pulled all these threads together when he wrote, "Besotted by the prostitute, robbed by the Jews, menaced by the worker, the Voltairean and masonic bourgeois begins to perceive that he is in a bad way. He has killed off every ideal and all faith within people's souls; he has corrupted everything around him, and all the corruptions he has sown are rising up before him like the avenging furies to push him into the deep."[30]

Drumont's paranoiac hallucination of the victimized middle-class male could stand as a plot summary of *Carmen* – it is even conceivable that Drumont was influenced by Bizet's opera. Just as "the Orient" imprinted itself on Hugo's dreams and thoughts "perhaps without his knowledge," so *Carmen* entered into the common consciousness and has shaped attitudes ever since its premiere. In the opera, Carmen herself represents virtually all available categories of alterity: inscrutable "Oriental," menacing worker, lawless criminal, *femme fatale*. And José, child of the Enlightenment bourgeoisie who surrenders his claims to racial, class and gender privilege because of her, must pay the consequences in the finale. Yet it is ultimately Carmen who pays – with her life – for José's identity crisis and Bizet's fantasies of alterity.

The lurid context from which *Carmen* originally emerged has retreated from us a bit: we may no longer link the opera's exotic elements with the colonized "Orient," insubordination with the Commune or female sexuality with syphilitic infection. And we do not like to remember the enterprises – colonial wars, genocidal purges of European ethnic minorities, massacres of striking laborers, increased regulation of women's bodies – that arose to counter nineteenth-century destabilization. But the opera continues to play along important faultlines of racial, class and gendered Otherness, however they may be construed at any given historical moment. Whatever else it is, *Carmen* is emphatically *not* a story about fate.

4 *The musical languages of* Carmen

All pieces of music develop in dialogue with many others. Far from being self-contained, a composition produces meaning through its use of codes transmitted and reproduced within a variety of repertories, its generic affiliations, the social contexts in which it is written and received, as well as through the strategic arrangement of its particular parts. This is true even of the most apparently autonomous of instrumental movements: its medium, formal procedures and aesthetic premises all have social histories, engaging associations that can neither be predicted in advance nor – even with the best of formalist intentions – kept altogether silent.[1] But it is more obviously true of a work such as *Carmen*, which operates in large part on the basis of its transgressive mixture of codes, genres and styles.

Bizet's first audiences recognized this transgressive mixture and responded accordingly (see Chapter 6). But because we no longer possess their expectations with respect to genre, we now tend to hear the opera as an unruptured entity: whether listening to the placid lyricism of Micaëla or the third-hand Cuban strains of the "Habañera," we hear only ... *Carmen*. Thus, before embarking on a reading of the opera itself, I want to sketch out some of the principal musical discourses it engages and juxtaposes.

Opéra-Comique

Carmen belongs to the genre of *opéra-comique*, and it must be read in part in terms of the conventions of that genre, even though Bizet virtually imploded the *opéra-comique* with this work. We know he was dissatisfied with traditional *opéra-comique* as he had inherited it from composers such as Boieldieu (see Chapter 2). But he was not seeking to invent a new dramatic form, nor was he aspiring to the terrain of the Opéra. In a letter to Ernest Guiraud he wrote, "Your place is at the Opéra; I'm afraid of making a poor showing there, of not having the necessary fullness. I shall shine at the Opéra-Comique; I shall enlarge and transform the genre."[2]

The typical Opéra-Comique audience was made up of middle-class patrons, and the elements of *opéra-comique* that appealed to these patrons were sentimentality, unambiguously moral plots, edifying characters and happy endings – precisely the elements Bizet violated in *Carmen*. The horror with which de Leuven responded to Bizet's plans (see Chapter 2) reveals how much the work ran counter to generic expectations. Why did Bizet insist upon setting this story as an *opéra-comique*, given that it was certain to offend its designated audience?

The defining characteristic of *opéra-comique* is spoken (rather than sung) dialogue. In the nineteenth century, most opera houses outside France demanded uninterrupted singing in the works they mounted; works with spoken dialogue either remained in the more limited venues for which they were designed or traveled abroad only after having been altered. Bizet was aware that all the spoken sections of *Carmen* would have to be converted into sung recitative if the work was to reach a cosmopolitan audience. He died before he could undertake the transformation himself, and thus Guiraud, his long-time colleague and friend, assumed the task of composing the recitatives in time for the premiere in Vienna in October 1875. Until quite recently, Guiraud's through-sung version was the only one available in performance, score or recording. Yet Bizet deliberately wrote *Carmen* with spoken dialogue, even though he knew this would mean revising it immediately for general consumption. He obviously considered *opéra-comique* the proper medium for the project.

The convention of spoken dialogue offers some crucial advantages. First, it makes possible more extensive and flexible interchanges among characters. Recitative, whatever its musical virtues, is cumbersome, restricting the amount of text that can be conveyed effectively. A comparison between the *opéra-comique* version of *Carmen* with the standard, through-sung score reveals that much more of Mérimée's text is retained in Meilhac's dialogues. We learn a good deal about Don José – his record of previous violence, his lack of interest in the local native women – in his spoken conversations with his superior officer. Because Guiraud had to compress or even eliminate most of this material, the new José appears more unambiguously as a naïf. Guiraud's version suffers from the musical demands of sung recitative.

Second, spoken dialogue permits the composer to exploit the difference between speech and song, and Bizet took full advantage of this feature of the genre. In the original version, for instance, Don José (unlike the other characters) only speaks through much of the first act. Since we know he is the leading tenor, his continued presence as a mere speaker whets our appetite to hear him sing. His reluctance to sing is, in fact, a crucial aspect of his persona: he holds on to speech except when impelled to move into singing through emotional excess – first when Micaëla reveals the letter from his mother, then when Carmen provokes him to passion. By contrast, Guiraud's José sings from his first entrance: even if his utterances become more impassioned at the crucial moments just mentioned, they fail to stand out as dramatic ruptures when surrounded by sung recitatives, as they do so strikingly when juxtaposed with flat speech.

Several other elements from the standard *opéra-comique* are utilized (and transformed) in *Carmen*. As was customary, the prelude presents an array of catchy tunes that show up later in the opera. This convention may reflect the continued influence of Weber's *Der Freischütz*, at the time still one of the most beloved operas in France and one of Bizet's lifelong favorites.

Moreover, two of the characters in *Carmen*, Micaëla and Escamillo, are based on standard types of the Opéra-Comique stage. As we have seen, Micaëla was introduced as a foil to Carmen, and her modesty, charm and stalwartness in the face of evil mark her as the stock *opéra-comique* heroine. She could easily be relocated within *La Dame blanche*, though in that context she would be the lead. Bizet offers us this character in *Carmen* (perhaps reluctantly), but then marginalizes her. Escamillo sports perhaps a bit too much exotic flair for the norm of *opéra-comique*, yet his boastful masculine prowess fits squarely within the genre. Georges, the dashing hero of *La Dame blanche*, performs a similar number about the thrills of military life, with enthusiastic responses from the chorus. Bizet himself seems to have regarded Escamillo's "Toreador Song" as a sop for the Opéra-Comique audience: he is reported to have said concerning this number, "So they want trash [*de l'ordure*]? All right; I'll give them trash."[3]

The chorus likewise is characteristic of *opéra-comique*, but again Bizet takes a convention (the inevitable presence of the chorus and its attendant spectacle) and makes it serve his own dramatic purposes. Chameleon-like, *Carmen*'s choruses represent a variety of social groups. Within Act I, the men are identified as soldiers and bourgeois loiterers, while the women are factory workers. This split helps to set up the class, gender and ethnic tensions between the two leads. But later, as Don José finds himself estranged from his initial context, the chorus becomes a unified social unit – gypsies or people attending a festival – against which his alienation shows up all the more starkly. Carmen, by contrast, always fits into and is supported by the community as represented by the various choruses.

Despite the alien elements discussed below, the musical style of *opéra-comique* dominates *Carmen*. Periodic phrases and symmetrical formal plans provide the normative base against which the disruptions of the drama unfold; and while Bizet's harmonic language in the nonexotic sections contains a few piquant shifts, it operates well within the expectations of standard French fare at this time. The opening chorus, for instance, indulges in a fashionably chromatic bass line that ruffles an otherwise placid context, and Micaëla's intrepid modulations in her Act III air show that she is not a mere creature of convention. But such harmonic strategies fit well within the bounds of *opéra-comique* as Bizet had inherited it. His genius resided not in his creation of new techniques, but in his ability to fit things together – literally to "com-pose."

The Wagner question

Carmen does not sound at all German to non-French ears. Indeed, one of the aspects of *Carmen* Austro-German audiences liked best was what they heard as its French lucidity, in striking contrast to their own music (see Chapter 6). Yet the testimony of French critics at *Carmen*'s premiere indicates that in its original context the influence of German music on Bizet's work was considered to be overwhelming.

Bizet's complex relationship with German music is easily documented. Like others of his generation trained at the Conservatoire, he was steeped in the music of Bach, Beethoven, Weber, Mendelssohn. His teacher Gounod was heavily influenced by German composers, especially Schumann, and Gounod encouraged him to study the Germans as models. Early in his career, Bizet wrote, "Next year I shall write something tragic and purely German. I shall finish perhaps by pleasing everyone or, rather, by pleasing no one."[4] Later he rhapsodized:

I am German by conviction, heart and soul, but I sometimes get lost in artistic houses of ill-fame. And I confess to you under my breath, I find infinite pleasure there. I love Italian music as one loves a courtesan ... Like you, I put Beethoven at the head of the greatest and most excellent. The Choral Symphony is for me the culminating point of our art. Dante, Michelangelo, Shakespeare, Homer, Beethoven, Moses! Neither Mozart with his heavenly form, nor Weber with his powerful and colossal originality, nor Meyerbeer with his mighty dramatic genius, can in my opinion dispute the palm with the Titan, the Prometheus of music.[5]

In this passage, Bizet reveals several fascinating attitudes to which we will return later in the chapter, especially his association of Italian music (and presumably other kinds of non-German music) and its pleasures with prostitution. For present purposes, it is sufficient to note his worshipful exaltation of German music, with which he wished to identify.

Beethoven stands as Bizet's particular idol. But by the 1870s in France, German style had become associated almost exclusively with Richard Wagner. Unconventional procedures were regularly branded as Wagnerian, and critics decried an epidemic of Wagner-worship in French composition: "Almost all of our young musicians aspire to the kiss of the modern Germanic muse, who seems to be too little the daughter of Apollo and far too closely related to M. Wagner and his cohorts. The result I would call the school of the *musical labyrinth*."[6]

Bizet was always quite ambivalent about Wagner, sometimes expressing admiration and other times contempt. When he first encountered Wagner's music, he wrote, "*There is absolutely nothing there*. They ... are the work of a man who, lacking melodic inspiration and harmonic inventiveness, has created eccentricity; extraordinary that this innovator should have no originality, no personality."[7] He later modified his position somewhat:

Wagner is no friend of mine, and I hold him in indifferent esteem; but I cannot forget the immense pleasure I owe to his innovating genius. The charm of his music is unutterable, inexpressible. It is voluptuousness, tenderness, love! If I played it to you for a week you would be infatuated! Besides, the Germans, who alas! are quite our equals musically, have understood that Wagner is one of their strongest mainstays. The German nineteenth-century spirit is made incarnate in that man.[8]

He also once described Wagner as "that great immense musician ... above and beyond all living composers."[9]

Throughout these years Bizet insisted upon his creative independence from Wagner: "Of course if I thought I was imitating
Wagner, despite my admiration, I would not write another note in
my life. *Imitation* is a fool's job. It is much better to write bad music
of one's own than other people's."[10] Yet Winton Dean has culled a
number of passages from Bizet's music that reveal the influence of
specific Wagnerian models.[11] And critics often accused him of
aping Wagner: "*Les Pêcheurs de perles* betrays on every page,
along with the talent of the composer, the bias of a school to which
he belongs, that of Richard Wagner. Everything M. Bizet has
written spontaneously bears the hallmark of really estimable
virtues. The rest is written by a disciple with his eyes on the
Master."[12]

What was at stake in the Wagner debate was clarified in a
sympathetic review by Théophile Gautier:

M. Bizet belongs to the new school of music and has broken away from
made-to-order arias, *strettos*, *cabalettas*, and all the old formulae. He
follows the dramatic action from one end of a situation to the other and
doesn't cut it up into little motifs easy to catch on to and hum when leaving
the theatre. Richard Wagner must be his favorite master, and we congratu-
late him on it. His aversion to four-square music, as boring as the
alexandrines of ancient tragedy, will perhaps earn him the reproach of a
lack of melody. But for this he will easily console himself. Melody does not
consist of waltzes and popular folk songs.[13]

Gautier claims, in short, that Bizet implemented certain Wagnerian practices as a means of opening up the stagnant, convention-
choked practices of *opéra-comique*.

The custom in *opéra-comique* of alternating between speech and
music results in a succession of discrete musical numbers. As
Winton Dean has written with respect to this feature, "The Paris
bourgeoisie liked its music broken up into small watertight compartments set in a framework of ordinary speech."[14] In the hands of
some of Bizet's colleagues, these "watertight compartments" can
seem quite tedious. The music is secured within symmetrical
packages, its energy prevented from leaking out into the "real
world" of dialogue.

In composing *Carmen*, Bizet repeatedly broke out of the traditional molds of *opéra-comique* procedure in ways that smacked of
Wagner's "endless melody" to French ears. Yet his models might
as easily have been earlier German music or even Italian opera – he
praised Verdi, for instance, although critics rarely accused him of

Verdi-worship. Whatever the models for his deviations, *Carmen* can scarcely be taken as anything other than a French work: while Bizet refuses to remain within "watertight compartments," he also refuses Wagnerian through-composition. He derives considerable strength from this middle position, for his most dramatic strategies are feasible only within an assumed framework of *opéra-comique*.

The opening sequence of each act follows the standard *opéra-comique* format: the scene is set through a crowd sequence, succeeded by a few balanced, self-contained numbers. But in each act, some event occurs that overwhelms this orderly succession and pushes into continuous, unpredictable action and music. Such continuity had always characterized the finales of acts – even in so restricted a work as *La Dame blanche*. But in *Carmen*, continuous activity erupts at other moments. Thus Carmen's entrance in Act I attenuates the symmetrical return of the refrain we expect. She destabilizes the established order, imposes one of her own and sends the formal dimension of the opera sprawling. In Act II, Don José's alien presence disrupts the easy sequence of gypsy songs. The struggle for power in José's and Carmen's love scene derives much of its strength from our expectation that it should be divided up into neat little chunks.

As we saw in Chapter 2, Bizet had to fight for these deviations: the librettists wanted a break for applause after José's "Flower Song," and the chorus and orchestra complained that the continuous sections were impossible to execute. Halévy confessed that he found the opera too complex, and many critics agreed (see Chapter 6). But even if *opéra-comique* audiences were the ones most likely to resist Bizet's formal innovations, they also were the ones best prepared to experience the effects he wanted to produce: the overthrow of an orderly universe by the violence of Carmen's encounter with Don José. It is precisely as an *opéra-comique* – albeit a heavily transformed and transgressive one – that *Carmen* creates its impact.

One of the characters in *Carmen* is a displaced "German," namely Don José. No one would mistake his music for German, of course, but he carries the burden of what was understood as German influence in the opera. It is he whose music always threatens to overflow its bounds with what Dahlhaus calls "lyric urgency,"[15] whose vision of his relationship with Carmen is "endless melody," whose discourse refuses the immediate gratification of what Gautier called the "popular folk songs" and "four-square music" of the more conventional characters. Not only does his own music violate norms of conventional propriety, as in the "Flower Song," but he constantly drags the number-oriented *Carmen* into the disarray and musical enjambement that collaborators, performers and critics found unintelligible. Along with Bizet, Don José might well claim: "I am German by conviction, heart and soul, but I sometimes get lost in artistic houses of ill-fame." And it is to those houses of ill-fame that we now turn.

"Exoticism" in *Carmen*

The exotic qualities in *Carmen* have been understood in a number of different ways. Many writers throughout its history have heard in the opera the very essence of Spain (or North Africa or the "Orient" – as we saw in Chapter 3, these locales were interchangeable under the ideology of Orientalism). As recently as 1987, Elaine Brody praised Bizet for his "natural instinct for the character . . . of Arabic music," in which she, following Hugo, specifically includes that of Spain.[16] To be sure, Bizet's representations of the exotic have to be recognized by listeners as "Spain" if the opera is to be intelligible. And to many of us, *Carmen* is as close to Spanish music as we ever get. As Brody writes in concluding her chapter on exoticism, "Some people believe that the best Spanish music has been written by French composers" (p. 76).

There are at least two major problems with such a position. First, it confuses the image of the ethnic Other concocted by the Northern European with the thing itself, then castigates the ethnic for failing to match the effectiveness of the caricature. Second, it mystifies how composers such as Bizet constructed images of "Spain" that seem so convincing (at least to everyone except the Spanish, who persist in hearing the whole opera as French). In matters of social discourse, "instinct" is not a sufficient answer.

Others try to explain the Spanish flavor in *Carmen* by referring to its use of actual Hispanic music. When composing *Carmen*, Bizet did a certain amount of homework, and a few of its numbers are based on materials gathered during his research. Bizet cited one of his sources in the original score: the "Habañera" (a dance from Havana) was based on the song "El Arreglito" by the Spanish composer Sebastián Yradier. Yradier had enjoyed a degree of visibility in Paris as the voice teacher of the Spanish-born empress. But although he was himself Spanish, he did not compose his exotic music as an expression of his own ethnic culture, but rather as an exercise in exoticism. For Yradier had traveled to Latin America, and the "Creole" musics he collected there formed the basis for his own pseudo-folk compositions, including the African-Cuban song Bizet borrowed for *Carmen*. We do not know how Bizet came to know this song (indeed, he seems to have taken it for a folk song at first), but Yradier's music appeared on programs in the *café-concerts* in which Céleste Mogador performed.[17] "El Arreglito" thus brings with it associations not with art music, but with the popular music of the Parisian cabarets: it belongs to a social milieu quite antithetical to that of the Opéra-Comique. This intrusion of music from "houses of ill-fame" on to the stage of the Opéra-Comique becomes one of the reigning tensions in *Carmen*.

The entr'acte to Act IV likewise has a quasi-Spanish pedigree. It is loosely based on a Spanish *polo* (an Andalusian genre) from Manuel García's *tonadilla*, *El criado fingido*. This *polo* appears in a collection later found in Bizet's library. Like Yradier, García was a collector and arranger of folk materials: any "authentic" Spanish flavor Bizet received from this source too was already heavily mediated. One more borrowing – the tune for Carmen's defiant line "Coupe-moi, brûle-moi" in her Act I interrogation – has been traced to a song from Ciudad Real.

These instances of specific models, however, fail to account for much of the exotic music in *Carmen*, most of which was freely composed. Some of Bizet's research into Spanish music may have been less formal, for such music was fashionable in Paris at the time. A critic of the premiere wrote: "It would have been easy for him to take one of the thousand Spanish melodies everybody is singing and playing on guitars, to have assimilated it more or less and interpolated it into his score."[18] Bizet's collaborator for *L'Arlésienne*, Daudet, listed among his own tastes in music "that of the Spaniards in the rue Taitbout," and he recorded his reactions to Hungarian gypsies: "The zigzag violin-bowings of the Tziganes kept me from seeing the Exposition. Each time those cursed violins caught me as I went by – impossible to go farther. I had to stay there until evening, a glass of Hungarian wine on the table, a lump in my throat, madness in my eyes, my whole body quivering to the nervous beat of the tympani."[19] Gautier's description of Bizet's music for the gypsy dance in *La Jolie Fille de Perth* (quoted below) echoes this portrait.

Despite the influence of actual Spanish, Spanish-American or gypsy sources, however, Bizet's agenda was not ethnography. He

liberally altered even his borrowed materials to fit his own purposes, and he composed "Spanish" numbers that only superficially
resemble indigenous music. As in *Les Pêcheurs de perles* or
Djamileh, the exotic passages in *Carmen* are first and foremost
products of Orientalism: they are fantasies about the Other firmly
grounded in French culture. Ernest Reyer (who set Du Locle's
libretto based on Flaubert's *Salammbô*) acknowledged as much in
his description of Bizet's Orientalist music in *Djamileh*:

Here we have true Oriental music, at least as it is understood by visitors to
the countries of its origin ... It is true, not through imitation of certain
instrumental effects *sui generis*, nor by the use of a scale wholly different
from ours, but by the accompaniment it gives to the landscape our
imagination evokes, of the picture it spreads before our eyes. It is ... a
truth that takes into consideration our ears and the nature of the musical
sensations to which we are accustomed. Besides, don't we know that all
music when it travels changes climate, loses its effectiveness by losing its
poetry, and sometimes even changes character?[20]

Bizet's "authentic" materials affect the overall fabric of his exotic
operas to the same extent that genuine "Oriental" motifs inform
Hugo or Ingres – they enhance the illusion of veracity, but only for
the French audience for whose pleasure the works are designed.
The framework remains nineteenth-century French culture and its
insatiable appetite for things exotic.

Within that context, a code had developed for the depiction of
the "Oriental" in music. Dahlhaus identifies some of the standard
characteristics of nineteenth-century European exoticism in music
as "pentatonicism, the Dorian sixth and Mixolydian seventh, the
raised second and augmented fourth, nonfunctional chromatic
coloration, and finally bass drones, ostinatos, and pedal points as
central axes."[21] I would add a few more: colorful timbral effects
(especially percussion), phrygian seconds, simple formal designs
and insistent dance rhythms.

Each of these characteristics bears some resemblance to genuine
non-Western musics. Yet in each instance, what is important is the
fact of deviation from the European norm. As Reyer pointed out,
the Orientalist composer "takes into consideration our ears and the
nature of the musical sensations to which we are accustomed."
Gautier indicates what was expected of musical portraits of gypsies
in his description of a dance interlude from Bizet's *La Jolie Fille de
Perth*:

the bacchanale of the gypsies, which recalls with unusual felicity those strangely passionate songs with their mad verve, harsh, savage, yet so sadly tender and melancholy, so nostalgically reminiscent of the *Zigeuner* ... M. Bizet has wonderfully understood the charming, wild poetry of this music, which, with all the colorful independence of the gypsy, joins voice to note and rejects any regulation of its caprice.[22]

These musical gypsies become recognizable through their display of standard ethnic stereotypes, the many ways in which they differ from *us*: strangely passionate expression, mad verve, harshness, savagery, sad tenderness, melancholy, charming wildness, colorful independence, unregulated caprice. These are characteristics identified forty-five years earlier in Hugo's *Les Orientales*, and they could describe Carmen herself. The actual signifying practices of ethnic musics matter little here, for what the European ear expected to hear in exotic music was it own image of difference: this music reinscribes not so much its ostensible musical model as European notions of what the Other is like.

Thus Bizet composed most of his "exotic" music not through instinct or by virtue of his borrowing from ethnic sources, but rather by means of this well-developed set of signs that he and his audiences shared, as do most contemporary listeners. When listening to foreign musics, the Western ear usually notices that some of the pitches cannot be justified on the basis of tonal scales. These points of difference then become crucial as marks of identification. A composer can give the impression of exotic music – to peers, at least – by salting the score liberally with these fetishized pitches. To a musician whose native music is thus being imitated, for whom such pitches ordinarily operate within a cohesive network of relationships, the result is nonsense; but to the European listener, the imitation may sound even more "authentic" than the original, for it delivers a concentrated image of "difference," purged of all those elements that might have been perceived neither as intelligible nor as satisfyingly exotic.

The characteristic pitch deviations in Orientalist music rarely penetrate below the surface of what otherwise is a thoroughly Western musical configuration. Thus, extensive melodic chromaticism may invoke the micro tonal inflections of some Eastern musics, but in exoticist music it operates (as in the "Habañera") within four-bar phrases and conforms to tonal logic at the cadences. Likewise, modal references may occur (as in the phrygian flavor of the "Seguidilla" or the entr'acte to Act IV), but genuine modal

procedures remain irrelevant. The tetrachord descent so characteristic of flamenco music permeates the opening number of Act II,
but its manipulation is pure Bizet: the first descent (E to B) pivots
without warning into another (B to F♯), followed by a colorful,
arbitrary alternation between F♯ and F♮ before sliding back
(without functional logic) to the tonic E. The listener is treated to
the thrill of illicit pitches, but is spared the burden of trying to
unravel an alien musical language.

Such devices serve the utopian function of permitting the imagination to escape the strictures of tonal rationality, but they simultaneously reinforce notions of the essential irrationality of the
exotic. The structures of Orientalist pieces are usually simplistic,
since complex formal processes are counted among the unique
accomplishments of the West. The static bass lines of much of this
music betray a Western belief in the timelessness, the lack of
interest in progress among "Orientals." But what the "Orient"
offers in exchange for progress and intellectual complexity is the
sensuality the West tends to deny itself. Orientalist scores exploit
color in place of the "purely musical ideas" that were the pride of
nineteenth-century Absolute music. They foreground timbres alien
to the standard orchestra or use the orchestra to mimic exotic
instruments, such as the guitar or sinuous, nasal winds, as in the
entr'acte to Act IV.

And Orientalist music tends to be animated through dance
rhythms – not rhythms that could be mistaken for European genres,
but rhythms calculated to engage the body in a very particular set of
physical responses. In describing the stereotypical gestures of
"exotic dance," Gautier wrote, "Swinging of the hips, twisting of
the body, head jerks and arm développés, a succession of voluptuous and swooning attitudes, such are the foundations of dance in
the Orient."[23] Mérimée's José describes his first impression of
Carmen in terms of her swaying hips, and these are the principal
elements of most of Carmen's music during the first two acts. The
rhythms of the "Habañera" or the "Seguidilla" routinely inspire
choreographers to demand sensual hip motion for these numbers in
performance, and the lyrics for the opening number of Act II even
describes such motions verbally. Carmen is thus identified through
her seductive body – the body that Don José tries to deny (witness
his chaste, mother-oriented exchange with Micaëla), but that
compels him to embark on his life of crime.

The mere fact that Carmen is depicted through dance would not be a problem, were it not for the mind/body anxieties so evident in late nineteenth-century French art and in Bizet's own life and documents. Carmen attracts José and the audience because of her easy relationship with her body, but she instills dread for the same reason (see section on prostitution in Chapter 3).[24] *Carmen* can be read as an indictment of the bourgeois fear of the body or as a moral lesson about the consequences of succumbing to the pleasures of the flesh. But in either case, Bizet does not have Carmen dance merely to gratify the ballet-loving Parisian public: her swinging hips – which are alien to ballet – are a crucial issue in the opera.

Thus it becomes necessary to pay close attention not only to Bizet's devices for fabricating the "exotic," but even more to the uses to which he puts them. As we have seen, the model Bizet used for his "Habañera" was neither gypsy nor Spanish, but Cuban. It was selected not for its presumed "authenticity," but for particular qualities – a descending chromatic line and the African-Cuban impulse of its genre – that fit his dramatic concept. Bizet reworked the rhythms of "El Arreglito" so as to match Gautier's description of "Oriental " dance, and he enhanced its sensuous melody so as to convey unambiguously the seductive character of Carmen.

Carmen's "Seguidilla" represents an even more complex fusion of codes and purposes. Its surface can be described in such a way as to make it seem like stock Orientalism: compelling dance rhythms, mysterious modal inflections, alternation between stasis and "irrational" harmonic moves. But here again Bizet has two goals: to give enough cues from his exotic code to persuade us that this music is "Spanish" (or "gypsy"), and to enact musically one of the central events in the opera – Carmen's seduction of Don José. Thus the melodic chromaticism signifies the "Orient," Carmen's beguiling treachery and perhaps also, by extension, the latent treachery of the "Orient." Her unpredictable harmonic shifts display the alterity of the "Orient" to Western logic, but they also create the snares into which José falls. Once lured into those moments of slippage, he cannot find his way out. Carmen calls the shots harmonically, psychologically and dramatically in this scene, but she conceals her motives behind the pretense of exotic dance.

Such double exploitation of exotic codes would not work without the time-honored association between "Orient" and "Woman."[25] It is noteworthy that Bizet gives the other potentially exotic characters besides Carmen (the cigarette girls, the male gypsies) relatively normative discourses not marked by the "Orient." Only

Carmen is characterized regularly through "Oriental" codes: she is the opera's bearer of exoticism *and* seductive femininity. Her signature – sometimes called the "fate motive" (see Chapter 5, Ex. 3) – presents both of these in concentrated form. Its identifying interval, the taboo augmented second, had been a stock emblem for the Oriental or the Jew for a very long time in European music. When the motive first makes its appearances within the opera proper, it accompanies Carmen's flamboyant, teasing entrance: even as she reveals herself in response to the pleading male chorus, her music marks her as an elusive, slippery *femme fatale*. As the events of the opera unfold, the motive becomes the sign of cruel fate itself, but it already has been marked as "Oriental" and seductress. To describe Carmen's music simply by labeling it "Oriental" or "Spanish" is not satisfactory, for such an explanation sidesteps the ideological implications of Orientalism and its closely related misogyny. For the musical fabric of *Carmen* is steeped in both of these.

Another dimension of Carmen's musical characterization must be discussed here: her discursive perversity. Unlike the other characters, who tend to remain within a single stylistic domain, Carmen is virtuosic in all of them. When she speaks to herself (as in the Card Scene) or in earnest (as in the final interchange with José), her utterances are unmarked – as though subjectivity were universal, unaffected by ethnicity or gender. But her public persona is semiotically promiscuous: she sings "gypsy" music, but always in such a way that she might be understood as simply performing cabaret numbers (which Bizet actually gives generic names: "Habañera" and "Seguidilla") rather than expressing herself; she can converse fluently in José's musical tongue and seduces him in the "Seguidilla" by dictating to him in his own histrionic style the terms of his passion; she sings duets with Escamillo; she banters with her fellow-smugglers. Like Mérimée's Carmen and the "alien-at-home," Bizet's heroine has mastered the languages of those around her and can slip easily in and out of them without revealing "herself."[26]

This aspect of Carmen's character kindles both fascination and suspicion. If Carmen were consistently just an "Oriental," she would not pose nearly so great a threat. Instead she slips unpredictably from the "exotic dance" of cabaret entertainments to high opera, throwing cultural boundaries of class, race and sexual propriety into confusion at a time when those boundaries were felt to be under siege. The Opéra-Comique was one venue where the bourgeoisie could expect to see its values mirrored unambiguously. The fact that Bizet defiled that stage with the music of the "Spaniards in the rue Taitbout," the working-class *café-concerts* and the showgirl accounts for much of the horror with which *Carmen* was received.

Winton Dean has insisted repeatedly that there is nothing "sordid" or "vulgar" about *Carmen*, but this is a position more easily maintained at a time when the sources of these musics and their attendant social associations are no longer alive. The mass culture from which Bizet borrowed so heavily for this opera represented the dreaded Other to the bourgeoisie:[27] regardless of the dignity Bizet may have given the character of Carmen, he drew much of her music from those depths of Parisian night-life that shocked his contemporaries.

Carmen revolved dramatically around the encounters among these discourses: between high art and the "degraded" entertainment music of the cabaret, between the sentimentality of *opéra-comique* and the "Realism" of contemporary literature, between "Oriental" and European, between French lucidity and Wagnerian excess. In a sense, Bizet aspires in this opera to the "vulgar": he had found the perfect vehicle for enacting the struggle between his weakness for "artistic houses of ill-fame" and the disciplining elements of his "German soul."

Narrative in nineteenth-century music

The fact that all these discourses are present in the opera does not mean that they carry equal weight, for the conventions of dramatic and musical narrative favor certain arrangements and outcomes. Standard Western narratives require both a protagonist and something that stands in contrast to that protagonist. Without a protagonist, a narrative would lack crucial dimensions such as identity and point of view, which help us to predict probable closure. But without the contrasting element, the plot that compels us through time would not materialize. The Other produces the desire necessary for narrative continuation, but it also constitutes an obstacle that must finally be subdued – congenially or forcibly – for the sake of closure.

In mainstream literature, the role of protagonist tends to be assigned to someone much like the artist – male, middle-class,

European – while the Other is designed to stand in dynamic contrast. Because romantic interest typically motivates plots, the Other is usually female, and closure occurs when the difficulties between the two forces dissolve, leading to marriage. The genre of *opéra-comique* was almost invariably arranged in this fashion, making it the ideal backdrop for engagement parties. Traditional tonality itself adheres to such a paradigm, as Schoenberg complained in his *Theory of Harmony*, just as he launched off into what we call – against his wishes – atonality:

For [our forebears] the comedy concluded with marriage, the tragedy with expiation or retribution, and the musical work "in the same key." Hence, for them the choice of scale brought the obligation to treat the first tone of that scale as the fundamental, and to present it as Alpha and Omega of all that took place in the work, as the patriarchal ruler over the domain defined by its might and its will: its coat of arms was displayed at the most conspicuous points, especially at the beginning and ending. And thus they had a possibility for closing that in effect resembled a necessity.[28]

To be sure, twentieth-century cultural forms have tried to escape the constraints of narrative precisely by avoiding plot, unified point of view and closure. Schoenberg argues in his *Theory of Harmony* for the possibility of permitting dissonances and tonal "vagrants" (i.e., musical gypsies) to survive rather than forcing them to submit to tonic. But in the nineteenth century, this standard narrative paradigm still exerted power over literary and musical forms, even though they were increasingly challenged by artists who balked at conforming to such conventions. Thus even when a nineteenth-century narrative deviates from the paradigm, it is still to be understood in tension with the expected norm if its violations are to be meaningful.

Don José fancies himself the protagonist of such a narrative. Even in their last encounter, he presents to Carmen his vision of a happy-ever-after ending to their tumultuous affair. His dream of closure demands, of course, her domestication, her submission to his authority; and to him (and the Opéra-Comique audience), this resolution would appear only proper. Carmen stands as his Other – not only in the subordinate position with respect to gender, but also with respect to race and class. Her triple alterity is evident from the beginning of Act I, which opens with a chorus of colonial soldiers guarding a native population of swarthy, working-class females. In almost every sense, power is located with the soldiers and José – they control the narrative frame.

Carmen proves to be a difficult force to contain, however. The desire she inspires overwhelms the narrative, dwarfing those members of the protagonist-team whose job it is to exploit and then subdue her energy. Her insistence on her right to agency threatens to wrest the narrative away from its conventional moorings, and her seductive cabaret tunes virtually hijack the opera, easily marginalizing the sentimental passion of José's more prestigious musical discourse. She injects elements of unpredictability, dissonance and chromaticism into the previously diatonic mix; and even if these scandalous elements require purging, the return to diatonicism after her advent becomes almost unimaginable. Like many a fantasy of the *femme fatale* in the second half of the nineteenth century, Carmen rises as a phantom too powerful to defuse through normal hegemonic means.

Yet despite Carmen's domination of the stage, she still occupies the subordinate position with respect to narrative. Far more is at stake in *Carmen* than this man and this woman: the nineteenth-century social order that had guaranteed the smooth unfolding of narrative relied upon shared assumptions concerning the "proper" power relationship between men and women, European and colonial, the middle and working classes, high and low art, consonance and dissonance. So long as none of these assumed relationships was challenged, the entire complex – gender, class, race, cultural prestige, narrative or musical propriety – could appear to maintain itself "naturally." But when a threat arose on any of these fronts, the response was often violent, violence in the service of social order.

In a nineteenth-century narrative, the bestowing of power on a sexually self-regulating, "Oriental," working-class cabaret entertainer can only be provisional. Likewise, the stripping away of the male protagonist's signs of privilege virtually demands violent backlash. For regardless of the relative charisma of the two principal characters in *Carmen*, the opera is still the product of male artists and institutions. The framework weighs against her – Carmen (herself an invention of those artists and institutions) is doomed before she begins. The chief question that remains open in the opera concerns the significance of José's final act. Without doubt he achieves closure: the musical excess that had been unleashed when José and Carmen met is laid to rest by means of her murder. Yet this closure scarcely stands as triumph.

Bizet's achievement lay in the fact that he took a schema so overloaded with issues, so overdetermined with respect to probable outcome, and created a work that has continued to engage and trouble audiences for over a hundred years. Only so much can be accomplished by examining the tributaries that fed into this opera, for these sources were available to all his contemporaries, none of whom matched Bizet's masterpiece. We turn now to *Carmen* itself.

5 Synopsis and analysis

Prelude (A major)

The prelude has three principal thematic sections, each of which reappears later in the opera in conjunction with specific characters or situations. It thus introduces highlights and also the affective tensions that compel the opera. By the time it returns in the final act, the prelude's various sections will have become so heavily thematized that it may be heard in retrospect as having contained the opera's central dramatic dilemmas. But when we first hear it, it serves a more immediate function: it establishes the opera's exotic; deceptively festive atmosphere.

The first section introduces the flashy, pseudo-Spanish music that returns in the Bullfight Scene of Act IV (Ex. 1). Two features of this segment seem noteworthy. First, it is composed of the four-bar phrases typical of *opéra-comique*. This regularity is violated only four times in the entire prelude. Yet the expectation of four-bar phrases becomes so ingrained that even a slight alteration constitutes a dramatic event. An extraordinary degree of order is set up by this phrasing – an order that is extremely resistant to change or difference.

Second, while each four-bar strain is static within itself, each pivots harmonically in its last measure – under a flamboyant trill – to the next segment, which sets out a contrasting key (A major, D major, A major, C major, A major). Here too we have a high degree of certainty, with the constant, reassuring returns to tonic. But the harmonic pivots – especially the move to the irrationally related C major – offer the thrill of the unexpected, even if they quickly retreat back to A major. The effect is bold, colorful, yet ultimately stable.

A contrasting section in F♯ minor follows the repetition of the opening. This too has a high level of redundancy, yet it also

Ex. 1

manages to create dramatic contrasts between its quiet beginning and aggressive second half, which leads back dramatically – under a crescendo of bravado flourishes – to the opening segment. This section too is insulated formally as the middle unit of a larger symmetrical structure. Moments of difference emerge only to be

Ex. 2

absorbed into balanced formal schemes. We thereby become conditioned to expect nested sets of Chinese boxes.

The next large unit – what we later come to identify as Escamillo's swaggering "Toreador Song" – helps to reinforce that pattern (Ex. 2). Once again we proceed with compulsive four-bar phrases, now in F major. And once again diatonic security is risked briefly as phrases move to the more somber D minor, then towards A minor/major and back to F major, where the whole complex repeats with more splendid instrumentation. The repeat follows the original plan until the final phrase, which remains centered around A major, facilitating a return of the prelude's opening unit. Another phrase irregularity occurs at this juncture: instead of the two-measure flourish that completed the requisite four bars the first time through, Bizet elides the conclusion of the "Toreador" material with the return of the beginning.

Neither these minimal phrase irregularities nor the seemingly innocuous modulations would be worthy of mention in discussions of most compositions. In *Carmen*, however, the tension between symmetry and transgression emerges as a central theme. Thus far, none of the deviations truly poses a threat to the prevailing order, for these colorful, localized surprises are easily absorbed. But the final segment of the prelude reveals the significance, the danger of this process. The prelude resembles Freud's game of "fort-da," in

Ex. 3

which a child experiments with feelings of separation and identity by tossing a spool on a string away ("fort") and then triumphantly retrieving it ("da"). But the prelude's final toss of the spool proves irretrievable.

Following what sounds like the confident final cadence, the prelude plunges into D minor with a fortissimo tremolo (Ex. 3). Time itself, which has been measured out in four-bar units, seems to stand still. Under the tremolo, a new motive emerges, a motive marked by the augmented second. This interval – defined as illicit in traditional counterpoint – has long been associated in Western music either with exotic Others (Jews, "Orientals," gypsies) or (in, say, the works of Bach) with extreme affective states such as anguish.

In *Carmen*, both connotations turn out to be crucial, and they continually play off one another as a kind of grim and deadly pun. For the motive will later be linked explicitly both to the gypsy Carmen and to Don José's fatal, anguished attraction to her. The motive also resonates with conventional musical semiotics of evil: the tremolo, diminished sevenths and foreboding timpani strokes greeting each presentation of the motive all descend from Weber's demonic imagery in *Der Freischütz*, one of Bizet's favorite works. But whereas Weber used them to refer to the devil, Bizet aligns them with the "Oriental" *femme fatale*.

As this segment unfolds, the motive repeatedly writhes its way to temporary points of rest, only to begin again on the new pitch level. At the end of the first phrase, the melody unexpectedly cadences quietly on F major. Immediately it starts over, again fortissimo and at a higher pitch, this time to be reined in on the irrationally-related key of Ab major. Following this cadence, the process reverses itself: the sinister motives rise from a quiet beginning, through increasing intensification to a crisis on a diminished seventh, which breaks off abruptly on to another diminished seventh, followed by ominous silence. This concluding dissonance occurs on the *fifth* measure of the phrase: the crisis overflows the normative four-bar boundaries that had managed up until now to govern even this traumatic episode. After all the cushioned protection of regular phrases and reliably returning opening materials, we find ourselves disgorged into a tonal, rhythmic and structural void.

This, then, is the shocking conclusion of what had been an obsessively symmetrical prelude. The "fort-da" game is violently ruptured, the security of the *opéra-comique* genre shattered. The dramatic action of the opera takes place within the breach that thereby opens up: the unresolved dissonance of the diminished seventh casts its shadow across the events as they unfold until the prelude-complex returns for its postponed closure in the last act. Given the constraints of nineteenth-century tonal form (as well as the demands of this specific piece, which relies so heavily upon symmetry and four-square order), this gaping wound – this violation of prevailing order – must eventually be healed or corrected, whatever the cost. All this before the curtain rises.

ACT I

Introduction: A square in Seville (B♭ major)

The next music we hear sidesteps the rupture and attempts a new beginning. Over a pedal on F, a swirl of sound develops and gradually channels us into a different world. If the various musical segments of the prelude always established their keys immediately, this number delays that certainty by resolving the pedal to its tonic B♭ only at the first cadence of the chorus – by which time we are heavily invested (musically, affectively, dramatically) in its processes. This strategy enhances the illusion of "realism," for the scene appears to take shape before our very ears. We are attracted into its realm as though by our own curiosity.

Whereas the music of the prelude announced its exotic affiliations without visual or verbal cues, the setting of this first number is discernible as Spain only by virtue of costumes, stage set and the designation "Seville" in the program. Otherwise, we might just as well be on a Parisian boulevard, for the music itself belongs not to the realm of the exotic, but rather to the "unmarked" discourse of contemporary French style. Nor is it sung by gypsies or characters construed as "Spanish," but rather by soldiers in an occupying army, present to police the domestic population. Their words underscore their sense of distance from the very "Spain" to which the prelude introduced us, as the soldiers sing of killing time by watching the local inhabitants who pass in the street. Their refrain, "Drôles de gens que ces gens là!" ("What odd people they are!"), makes it abundantly clear that they are not to be confused with the natives. Even if they are ostensibly a Spanish army, they are of a significantly different class and ethnic constituency. They derive pleasure from gazing at the Other from positions of social privilege.

In this, they resemble the audience. The opening number expressly legitimates distanced, objective, voyeuristic observation as we viewers are invited likewise to gaze unabashedly at "these odd people." Without necessarily noticing how, we enter into the opera's dramatic events from the soldiers' point of view. They naturalize spectatorship and situate us with the dominant social group that watches with amusement the colorful antics of the gypsies from the sidelines.

Thus it is crucial that the soldiers sound like "us" rather than like "them." They sing in a fashionably bored manner, casually sporting sophistication through chromatically inflected lines and clever Neapolitan eruptions of mock surprise at cadences. They are not especially memorable – theirs is not the music we go away humming, and it sounds quite pale in the wake of the brilliant prelude. But this only makes the chorus more effective. As our stand-ins, they are transparent; we listen *past* them to the spectacle they offer for our delectation.

Like the prelude, this opening number is composed of nested symmetries. After the chorus has presented the principal materials, Moralès (one of the dragoons) throws in a brief contrasting section that flirts with G minor. But the chorus returns immediately, bringing with it thematic and tonal security. Likewise, the chorus returns intact at the end of the scene. Thus even though the scene presents a radically different social and musical world from that of the prelude, it operates according to similar structural premises. If the prelude exploded at the end and wrecked its symmetries, we are here offered an alternative that promises secure returns. And for at least this scene and the next, the promise holds.

But it seems then that we have two competing frames for the opera, one identified with the Spanish-gypsy contingent ("them") and the other with the colonizers ("us"). The prelude has already heralded catastrophe. By beginning again with the cool, distanced *boulevardiers*, we are invited to understand the opera in terms of French objective rationality and its attendant *opéra-comique* discourses, rather than gypsy "fatalism." Both frames are crucial to the unfolding of the opera, for it is not only the audience that is disoriented by these contradictory modes of observation but also, of course, Don José, who cannot decide whether to stay in his position of social privilege or to give in to the appeal of the exotic. The ambiguities in the opera are in large part a result of Bizet's subtle double exposition.

The nested symmetries in this number recall the formal procedures of the prelude, but on a more pragmatic level, these symmetries permit Bizet to accomplish the furthering of plot within the context of sustained musical tableaux. For between the opening and closing segments of this scene, we are first introduced to some of the opera's central characters. This strategy operates throughout the opera; it is what allows *Carmen* to have such a high density of "hit tunes" and yet such compelling theatrical drive. The relationship between embedded action and frame is central to Bizet's higher-level dramatic strategy, for the embedded material and its

Ex. 4

tensions always threaten to overwhelm the frame – as already occurred once, at the end of the prelude.

The content of the embedded music in this first number involves Micaëla, a young girl who has known Don José since childhood and whom José's mother wants him to marry. She is sanctioned many times over (her modest behavior, the mother's approval) as the bourgeois feminine ideal. Yet when she first enters the scene as an unknown woman, she is perceived as simply female, and the soldiers (with Moralès in the lead) immediately start to solicit her. Their definition of "drôles gens" very much includes women. Micaëla is marked by Bizet too as just another woman, for her entrance is accompanied by the kind of slinky chromaticism that later signals Carmen's "dangerous" sexuality (Ex. 4). As Moralès tracks her movements ("Voyez, elle tourne, elle hésite"), the rising bass reveals the prurient interests of her spectators.

But from her first sung utterances, it is clear that the soldiers have read the signs inaccurately: she is shy but direct, and she refuses to be distracted from her mission. Although Micaëla was forced on Bizet and his collaborators by the Opéra-Comique management, they did not portray her as simple or humorless. At one point she surprises the soldiers by engaging in their banter. Moralès and his chorus have given her a parody of a military march in E major to inform her that José will arrive for the change of guard. They try to detain her, but she resists their advances and turns the tables: she mimics their own words (and key) in announcing that she will return for the change of guard, and then escapes by leaping to G major. Having lost their target, the soldiers drift back from their heightened keys and affect to the boredom of their cruising and their B♭ chorus, thus rounding out the musico-dramatic action.

We learn during the course of this interchange that Micaëla has the purest of motives. Yet the mere fact of her presence proves to be disquieting. It throws into flux the tonal stability that this male community had sustained up until her entrance: not only is she a foreign element, but she tempts Moralès to try to ensnare her in remote keys, and she escapes by substituting her own keys. But without Micaëla's destabilizing influence, the scene would have no dramatic content. We are dependent on "noise" of this sort for amusement, even though that noise challenges certainty. In this instance, the disturbance was but an innocuous flirtation, and the routine of the soldiers' world quickly returns.

This reading assumes the soldiers' point of view, in which Micaëla functions as a passing dissonance. Yet it is also possible to identify with her position as a potential victim in an alien terrain. Bizet gives us plenty of musical grist for such an interpretation, including Moralès' duplicitous ploys and the increasingly aroused exclamations of his chorus. Had she not escaped, Micaëla would have been subjected to continued harassment or even assault (see the discussion of Rosi's *mise-en-scène* for this passage in Chapter 7). But she manages to flee, and the formal return to the beginning chorus buttons us back into the dominant point of view – that of the soldiers who represent and ensure structural normality. Micaëla is temporarily forgotten.

Still, the sexual politics of this scene (which helps set the terms against which the rest of the opera will be heard) are complex. Micaëla is variously a temptress (she inspires lust, simply by virtue of being female), a tease (she arouses, then frustrates their desires) or the innocent victim of unsolicited advances. And the soldiers can be read as aggressors, as victims whose desires are inflamed and then frustrated, or as just regular guys. If so simple a scene is this slippery, then the addition of José and Carmen – both of whom are far more complicated than Moralès and Micaëla – will escalate the level of ambiguity exponentially.

As though to underscore the themes of voyeurism and the *femme fatale*, an early draft of the opera included at this point a pantomime – described cynically by Moralès – in which an old man is cuckolded by his young wife. This section was designed in response to the original actor playing Moralès, who demanded a fuller part, and it appeared only in the 1875 vocal score – not in the orchestral version. Accordingly, it is rarely performed.

March and Chorus of Street Urchins (A major; D minor)

The world of the *flâneurs* is disrupted by bugle calls, signaling the changing of the guard and promised advent of Don José. But the march that introduces him seems calculated to undermine the gravity of the military presence: its piccolo sonority and grace notes mark it as cute, not authoritative. And the central presence onstage is a swarm of street urchins mimicking soldierly behavior, further trivializing the dignity of the troop when it eventually appears.

A motivating factor for this scene may have been the tastes of the Opéra-Comique patrons, for the children's march offers a charming spectacle. Its perky music helps to delay the return of the conflicts foreshadowed in the prelude, as well as the entrance of Carmen. Once again the music unfolds in predictable four-bar units. And once again the plot itself is furthered in a dialogue sandwiched between two presentations of the children's march, a dialogue during which Moralès tells José that Micaëla is looking for him.

This dialogue is the first passage in the opera in which we encounter marked differences between the *opéra-comique* version and the one rearranged for grand opera with recitatives by Ernest Guiraud. Guiraud's version has Moralès and José sing their exchange, as the orchestra paraphrases Micaëla's "Mon brigadier ... Le connaissez-vous?" He thereby underscores through added music the connection between this and the previous scene, which we probably do not need. Bizet's version introduces Don José not with his heroic tenor voice, but through flat, everyday speech.[1] In both versions, the march returns; but as the regiment disperses, the children lose interest in the march, and the orchestra plays it alone to the end, fragmenting it wittily along the way.

In the dialogue preceding the next number, two crucial bits of information are conveyed: Zuniga (José's lieutenant) pruriently questions José about the girls in the cigarette factory, and José identifies Micaëla as a girl from home. Once again Bizet's and Guiraud's versions differ. Under sung recitative, Guiraud's orchestra recalls previous material – Micaëla's passage already cited during the earlier recitative and also standard figures representing feminine wiles, similar to the segment introducing Micaëla cited in Ex. 4. Bizet calls for no orchestral comments, but relies exclusively on speech.

Moreover, the *texts* of the two versions are not alike. Not only has the sung exchange been radically pared down to accommodate the relative inefficiency of recitative, but Guiraud's text has been cleaned up: his José declares his love for Micaëla and neglects to mention that he once killed someone. By contrast, Bizet's José quotes directly from Mérimée: he reveals his history of violence and remains noncommittal with respect to Micaëla (who is not in Mérimée). In both versions, he distances himself from the other soldiers, who pass their time ogling passers-by.

Chorus and Scene (C major; E major)

As though on cue, José's description of the factory workers brings them onstage, over a dominant pedal that breaks off in anticipation. But the music that arrives on the tonic after the dominant bears no resemblance to the hazy, undulating stuff that began the number. It shifts meter (6/8 to 2/4), and a male chorus again situates us in the position of voyeurs. This short introduction to the women's chorus resembles the opening number stylistically, insofar as both are marked by the chic harmonies one might expect to hear in a light musical revue.

The dominant pedal begins again, this time (as though through heightened expectations) in E rather than C major. Over this introduction, the men languish in recitative that descends by half-steps to an urgent seventh that remains unresolved. The emerging musical image serves several functions at once: it represents both the smoke rings of the cigarettes and the illusory nature of love vows to which the girls refer in their lyrics. It also simulates erotic trance and the elusiveness of women (especially as they slip enharmonically into flat keys and back again without warning). The cross accents blur metric certainty, producing an erotic swaying quality against expected impulses. Note that smoking was deemed improper for women in the nineteenth century; but prostitutes often smoked to announce their trade, as does Mérimée's Carmen when she accepts a cigar from the French narrator. The imagery in this scene thus signals the sexual availability of these women – if their status as working-class women of color is not sufficient.

This chorus too, like the previous numbers, obeys laws of closure, and it reaches a serene cadence that easily contains its quality of elusiveness.[2] The men, however, are not gazing randomly: they begin to clamor for "Carmencita." When we first meet Carmen, she is the third in a chain of female entities (Micaëla, the factory girls) who have been approached by the male idlers and – incidentally – offered up for our delectation. In both previous instances, the women played along, resisted or remained aloof, but they never threatened the control of the masculine community that secured each scene. Carmen's entrance, however, initiates a pattern of overflow, excess and damage that cannot be so easily recontained.

In fact, we have already encountered this character in another incarnation: the vampish flourishes that accompany her advent (Ex. 5) are but the speeded-up version of the augmented-second motive that spelled "Oriental," evil and anguish when we first met them at the end of the prelude. Now these meanings have added to them the dimension of "Woman." Carmen turns out to be the disruptive factor that derails the certainty (structural and patriarchal) of both prelude and first act. She is also the factor that brings into collision the two parallel expositions (the first exotic, the second "domestic" or neutral) that have been traced thus far. The triviality and conformity of the first three numbers of the opera may have lulled us into forgetting our first frame. If Carmen ruptures both procedures, her appearance in this second track also suggests the eventual fulfillment of that prior, more fearful symmetry – the inexorable return of the fatal stuff that seemed to have been abandoned in horror at the conclusion of the prelude.

For her first utterance, Carmen picks up the question posed by the men ("Quand je vous aimerai?") and also their F minor tonality. But she quickly takes control of both tonality and the right to sexual aggression. She toys with expectations by harmonizing the

Ex. 5

pitch f – which they had extended so hopefully – in as many ways as possible: she displays herself in Db major with a languorous melodic arch up to f^2, then subtly pivots and arouses the desire for Bb major, before slamming the door with her refusal in an unambiguous D minor (the key of the "fate" segment of the prelude). Unlike the previous three numbers – in which plot advancement occurred in the middle, only to be formally contained by the return of opening materials – this recitative leads directly into the next number, the centerpiece of Act I: Carmen's "Habañera."

Habañera (D minor)

The "Habañera" is the first number in *Carmen* based on materials not originally by Bizet himself. It seems to have been worked out in close collaboration between Bizet and Galli-Marié, the original Carmen, who was dissatisfied with the first several drafts.[3] Bizet modeled this – perhaps the most celebrated melody in the opera – on a Cuban-style song by a Spanish composer who was then popular in the cabarets (see Chapter 4). It lends a touch of "authentic" (rather than concocted) exoticism, even if its African–Latin origins scarcely seem appropriate for an opera set in Seville. Yet Bizet's lack of interest in imitating the "correct" ethnic musics does not betray a lack of discrimination. He was concerned with the *aura* of exoticism and with the affective or rhetorical consequences of his choices. And in these areas, his level of artistic discernment was extremely high.

Thus it is no accident that Bizet chooses to introduce his title character by having her perform a Cuban-style cabaret tune. Most of Carmen's utterances are numbers typical of entertainments at Lillas Pastia's establishment, even when she treats the idlers or (later) Don José to ad hoc performances. This creates a basic ambiguity in her dramatic construction: when she sings, does she express herself, or is she just performing a number? Do we ever have access to "Carmen herself," or only to a stage persona? Does Bizet deprive her of interiority by giving us a cabaret gypsy, or are we to understand that she strategically conceals herself behind her public image?

In interpreting the opera, much depends on whether one regards the "Habañera" as the rendition of a song for the pleasure of admirers who know Carmen as a popular performer or as the self-presentation of Carmen the woman. On the one hand, the entire community joins in enthusiastically on her refrains during this number, leaving only Don José as a nonparticipant. In the opening scene at Lillas Pastia's in Act II, we will witness much less ambiguously Carmen's interactions with her fans following her gypsy dance routine.

But on the other hand, we are encouraged to learn who Carmen is from the "Habañera": like José, we have no other source of information. At the very least, we know Carmen is accustomed to displaying herself within the public sphere, whether as performer or prostitute – or both. The song's persona freely celebrates sexual pleasure and promiscuity, although she reserves the right to choose (as does Carmen). At some level, the "Habañera" remains the song-and-dance number its generic title suggests; but its undecidability is central to the unfolding of the plot.

The affective tone is set before Carmen begins to sing. An instrumental vamp sets up and maintains an African–Latin rhythmic impulse that engages the lower torso, inviting hip swings in response. She thus makes us aware of her body in the context of a genre – *opéra-comique* – that usually offers evidence of physicality only through highly sentimentalized guises. Carmen's number is further marked by chromatic excess, as her melodic line teases and taunts, forcing the attention to dwell on the moment – on the erogenous zones of her inflections (Ex. 6).

Ex. 6

For instance, her descent by half-steps through the tetrachord d^2-to-a^1 is arranged so that we grasp the outline she implies (and thus are invited to desire the suggested outcome); as she moves through that descent, she alternately coaxes and frustrates. What is set up as normative rhythmic motion from d^2 to $c\sharp^2$ is halted on $c\natural^2$, where she plays with our expectations not only by lingering, but also by reciting in irregular triplets that strain against the beat. The $b\natural^1$ that follows is quick, suggesting that she will descend immediately to the expected goal; but the bb^1, which ought to have been a mere passing-note on a weak pulse, is given an insinuating nudge by the declamation of "*re*-belle." While there is never any question of tonal or melodic orientation in this phrase, her erratic means of descending through the tetrachord (and, subsequently, the remainder of the scale) reveals her as an expert in seductive rhetoric. She knows how to hook and manipulate desire. In her musical discourse, she is slippery, unpredictable, maddening, irresistible. Or at least this is the nature of her song.

At the cadence of her verse, the mode switches suddenly to D major, with the vamp still solidly grounded on the same tonic. The chorus comes in to repeat her opening lines, while she voluptuously sings the single word "l'amour." She then introduces a refrain ("L'amour est enfant de Bohême"), which, while it is more diatonic and straightforward, still offers opportunities for suggestive inflections. The chorus repeats this refrain, following which the vamp returns to D minor for the second verse, a repetition of the chorus and the refrain. Within its own confines, this number is as self-contained as any of the previous ones – perhaps even more so, given that the vamp remains on D throughout. But the provocative eroticism of the "Habañera" makes it a kind of Pandora's box. And its energies spill out immediately – *attacca* – into the next scene, the first yet that is not organized as a symmetrical set-piece.

Scene (A minor; A major)

At first it seems that we have returned to the male chorus that introduced Carmen. Again they press her to choose one from among them. But their excitement level is now higher – A minor rather than F – and instead of the jaunty cadence they presented her with before, they intensify their urgency, leading into the catastrophic music that concluded the prelude. The prelude's motive is, of course, the same as Carmen's flirtation, but with intimations of doom. During this passage, Carmen approaches Don José (the only one who had ignored her performance), taunts him about his *épinglette*, takes a flower from her bodice and – as the music breaks off on its diminished seventh – throws the flower at him. The women in the chorus laugh mockingly and repeat the "Habañera" refrain, "L'amour est enfant de Bohême."

In the remaining seventeen measures of the scene, as all but Don José leave the stage, the orchestra comments through a style that has not yet been evident in the opera – that of romantic lyricism (Ex. 7). As it turns out, this is José's mode of expression, although he has yet to sing a note. Yet this instrumental outburst give us access to José's subjectivity: his yearning, his turmoil, his passion. In an opera that has been exclusively concerned with exteriors and public exchanges, this is an extraordinary moment. As in film scores, this passage subtly arouses our sympathies and aligns them

Ex. 7

with José. The outburst gradually dies down into its component
parts: Carmen's motive coupled with José's half-step appoggiaturas
of longing. If it was already clear that the prelude motive represented "Oriental" and feminine wiles, its affective association with
anguish is here fatally engaged. For it is only through his anguish

that José can make contact with Carmen's signs. He experiences his own misery in the same musical terms that mark her racial and sexual Otherness, and that uneasy bond will destroy them both.

Unlike previous scenes, this one resembles a grab-bag; yet it is also the most important with respect to the multiple strands of the narrative structure. It offers two abortive attempts (the men's chorus, the "Habañera" refrain) at enacting the closure thwarted by Carmen's entrance; it engages directly with the tragic materials from the end of the prelude, thus linking back and pointing forward with considerable foreboding; and it introduces the stylistic voice of a new character, whose feelings we can share without verbal mediation. If José enters late into this complex, his music represents "universal subjectivity." And the issue of whose frame (Carmen's, with her ties to the prelude; the idlers', with their distanced irony; or José's, with his romantic passion) will regulate this opera becomes critical.

The link between this scene and the next differs in the two versions. Bizet records José's reactions to Carmen's floral assault through spoken dialogue taken from Mérimée: he compares her to a cat who only comes to those not interested; he posits that if there are witches, she is one. Micaëla enters, and as soon as she has made her presence known, they begin the next number. Guiraud, however, sets this passage as recitative. Along the way, he punctuates José's utterances with snippets of the previous scene, so as to impress firmly in our ears the principal musical and narrative motives: Carmen's flirtation, its transformation into the "Oriental"/anguish motive of the prelude (as he inhales the flower's fragrance) and the refrain line of the "Habañera." Micaëla's entrance pulls him abruptly, enharmonically, from the flat keys into which his thoughts had strayed. The musical figure that will accompany the maternal kiss in the following scene eradicates all traces of Carmen.

Guiraud's version thus accomplishes a good deal with respect to the contradictory forces that have been set into play in the opera, while Bizet's remains stark, musically uninflected. Yet the Bizet offers one crucial advantage: even in the face of Carmen's confrontation and his inner turmoil (as marked by the orchestra), José's singing voice remains unsounded in Bizet's original. In his version, we are still waiting to see what finally will push him – our romantic lead, our heroic tenor – into lyricism. Because Guiraud has José sing repeatedly in recitatives, he loses this powerful element of psychological development and suspense.

Duet (Bb major; G major)

José bursts into song for the first time with the words "Parle-moi de ma mère!" ("Tell me about my mother!"), which he utters twice, the second time rising urgently to high g. The passion he has kept bottled up thus far is revealed as intense and quickly provoked, though still attached to his mother. Or it may be that he seizes the memory of his mother as a safeguard against the actual *provocateuse* of his passions, Carmen (he implies this in his monologue in the middle of the scene). In any case, his outburst matches stylistically the orchestral surge ending scene v; if there was any question about whom the surge belonged to, this utterance removes all doubt.

Throughout this scene, Micaëla plays two roles that are carefully fused into one: she represents José's mother (in her descriptions of and direct quotations from that icon of José's affections) and also herself – although this latter role is clearest in her shy hesitations ("Et puis . . ."). During the course of the scene, she gives voice to her own sentiments only as they are masked safely either as the expression of the maternal love she has been requested to convey or as echoes of José's responses to that maternal love. In both cases, her feelings are woven together with those of the mother. She renders herself transparent, inaudible; she serves as the mother's conduit and stand-in, and she is successful precisely to the extent that her love is indistinguishable from the mother's. While passionate, her discourse is comforting, nurturing, chaste. The coy timidity with which she broaches the subject of the "maternal" kiss reveals the blend of prudery and titillation typical of treatments of sexuality in this day, especially for bourgeois audiences. The contrast with Carmen's frank carnality could not be stronger.

Micaëla's monologue is worth examining in some detail, for it represents the "normative" discourse of *opéra-comique* that is threatened in this opera by the more exciting music of gypsies, smugglers, cabaret singers and bullfighters. Although the key of Bb major has just been established, Micaëla begins formally ("Votre mère") over an Eb triad, thus quickly signaling religiosity (she invokes the "Amen" progression), and then moves to the unexpected harmonic shift that opens the second portion of her speech.

Ex. 8

tu lui di-ras   que sa   mè - - re   Son-ge

nuit et jour_____   à l'ab - sent,_____

Qu'el - le re-grette et qu'elle es - pè - re,   Qu'el - le par-

Here (in G minor) she starts quoting the mother's own words, beginning with a mincing imitation of the older woman's style. But as the mother's words approach the focus of her request – her José, her "enfant" – she becomes increasingly passionate (or at least Micaëla does in her relay of the conversation, for Micaëla stops marking the difference between herself and the mother). This surge results in a climax, after which she brings the statement back under control for a somewhat melancholy cadence in D minor. The d^2 of this cadence, however, melts into B♭ major for the core of the monologue: the segment in which the mother's message to José is communicated.

Several signs of bourgeois sentiment are brought to bear in this passage (Ex. 8). Harps arpeggiate throughout, both to underscore the poignancy of the utterance and to animate the harmonies unfolding slowly towards their projected goal. While the tonal plan of the speech is suitably modest (it goes to the dominant, then returns), each of its phrases contributes to its restrained urgency. Thus the opening phrase invests its first chord-change with double appoggiaturas, and its conventional cadence on V of V is rendered "meaningful" by the delayed arrival of c in the bass. The second phrase indulges in the poignant minor triads available within the diatonic complex before resolving on to the dominant and a triumphant f^2. Micaëla then moves for the bottom line: the mother's request that she convey a kiss to José. As she pivots towards this moment, harmonic certainty is thrown temporarily in question with a D major triad, only to melt back into B♭ and the push for the final cadence, which is capped just before resolution by the climactic g^2, the promise of which has fueled the monologue.

Micaëla thus manages to achieve the impression of vision and transcendence through her control of tonal impulses and postponed gratification, which is eventually granted in full. Unlike Carmen, who strives either for hypnotic harmonic stasis (as in the "Habañera") or for apparently arbitrary chromatic shifting (as becomes clear in subsequent scenes), Micaëla is a properly trained, goal-oriented bourgeois subject in her speech. Her libidinal urges are carefully channeled in accordance with the rationality of Enlightenment syntax. José bursts in at this point, inspired once again by reference to his mother ("Un baiser de ma mère!"), matching Micaëla's climactic pitch in his excitement. The kiss itself takes place during a four-bar orchestral interlude, which is marked by coy inflections and appoggiaturas: a tortured passage that attempts to convey emotional intensity and chastity at the same time.

José then begins the G major duet with recollections of his mother and village. After the rapturous build-up, his style is strangely bland: while still partial to high melodic pitches, he seems at least temporarily content. The accompaniment contributes a cradle-like rocking motion and a rustic horn call. Only the cadence itself deviates in any way from the expected, as his leading-tone f♯[1] is harmonized with a B minor triad. This slight destabilization is soon rectified as Micaëla enters to guide him back to G major. But as they approach the next cadence, they transcend together the various more obvious options and push up to a♭, to a♮ and a flooded release back to G major. The diatonicism that had appeared so unruffled at the beginning of the duet is rendered meaningful only as it is jeopardized and confidently reembraced.

At this moment, José recalls Carmen's flirtatious theme over its disorienting diminished seventh, but his memory of the maternal kiss rescues him. (In *Der Freischütz*, Max too calls upon his mother and chaste girlfriend to help him confront the ultimate evil of the Wolf Glen. By the late nineteenth century, however, evil is more strongly associated with female sexuality than with imaginary demons.) Micaëla jars him from his inner struggle. Before she returns home, José reprograms her, now as a conduit of his affections for his mother. He reiterates Micaëla's message in B♭, and together they repeat their duet to close the scene. The symmetrical order so disrupted by Carmen's entrance seems secure once again: her influence is recalled in the center of this complex, but is apparently dispelled when José recalls his mother.

In the short segment preceding the next scene, Micaëla departs, and José reads in the letter that his mother wishes him to transfer his emotions to Micaëla. In Guiraud's version, the whole B♭ passage is replayed (in A major) as José reads, then vows his obedience. But the final cadence is unsettled by the diminished seventh that represents Carmen, as José recalls her flower in order to announce his victory over its power. Alas, the flower and the diminished seventh open the door to his doom, which quickly unfolds in the following scene. Bizet's version returns José to his usual rational spoken discourse, which is interrupted by the sounding of the alarm. Once again, Guiraud underscores motivic connections to ensure that the listener grasps the struggle between the mother/Micaëla side and Carmen, while Bizet continues to exploit the stark contrast between the realism of spoken delivery and the hyperreality of the music.

Chorus (F♯ minor)

José's reverie is shattered by screams and piercing trills, high in the violins. An agitated introduction (again over a dominant pedal) pitches us forward into a quarrel among the factory women. A knife fight has occurred; one faction assigns responsibility to Carmen, the other faction, to Manuelita. Each group strains to persuade Zuniga, who here represents civic authority, to its point of view. Up until this scene, Bizet has solved the problem of satisfying the demands of both musical coherence and dramatic continuity by interjecting action sequences into the middle of what otherwise remain balanced musical units. The compulsive symmetries of most of the previous numbers are the result. But in this chorus, Bizet manages to integrate the exigencies of both music and drama in a way that is virtuosic and highly effective: here the set-piece itself furthers the action and contributes essential bits of plot information.

The vivid image of tussling women is accomplished through the agitated orchestra, the competition between the two choruses (who follow upon one another in rapid fire, raising the ante by heightening pitch level) and surface chromaticism that threatens tonal security. Yet this material is actually highly controlled: it sticks fast to F♯ minor, and while the imitative texture gives the impression of chaos, the alternations are quite orderly. The debate even follows the symmetrical patterning of previous sections: following the pause in which Zuniga orders José to investigate, the fight returns, providing our standard ABA structure. The women conclude, rather unexpectedly, on a triumphant F♯ major triad. As José leads Carmen from the factory, the orchestra appeals once again to the motive earlier associated with José's anguish (see Ex. 7) and winds down to an ominously subdued cadence on F♯ minor. In the ensuing dialogue, Zuniga queries José and then addresses his questions to Carmen herself.

Song and Melodrama (A minor)

As Zuniga interrogates Carmen, she refuses to respond directly to his questions. Rather she answers him with a taunting refrain, "Tra la la la la," to which she appends statements in which she variously dares him to torture her or sings suggestively of her lover, thus compelling her interrogators to think of her in sexual terms. Zuniga understands her scheme: he acknowledges his attraction as he flirts back, but exercises his power by ordering José to take her to prison.

The differences between Bizet's and Guiraud's versions are perhaps at their most critical in this scene. Bizet's is set as a *mélodrame* in which Zuniga speaks and Carmen replies by singing a song. Not only is the song she sings insolent (as it is in Guiraud's recitative setting as well), but the mere fact that she *sings* rather than speaks in response to legal interrogation represents intolerable behavior in itself. She deliberately employs an alien discursive mode, in order both to trivialize the exchange and to exploit the manipulative, erotic dimension of her music. We already know that she is a professional singer. She brings the world of the cabaret in to mock this austere realm. In Guiraud's version, everyone always sings, and the effect of this subversive intrusion of song is severely blunted.

Like the "Habañera," this song is marked as belonging to the world of the gypsies (Zuniga identifies it as "bohemian"). It flaunts the same quality of physicality as Carmen's previous number, but it has a strange modal flavor reminiscent of flamenco music: thus her opening phrase hovers suggestively between E minor and A minor, never really deciding on either. Not only does she resist legal circumscription, but she refuses to be nailed down tonally as well. Subsequent phrases move into C major (where she pretends to be yielding), and in her final version (sung with "impertinence while gazing fixedly at Zuniga") into E minor. After this departing shot, various solo instruments take up her taunt, concluding the scene with this motive squirming around A as an uneasy phrygian tonic with half-steps on either side.

An extensive dialogue follows. Zuniga leaves Carmen in José's keeping while he goes to obtain the charge for her arrest. No sooner are they left alone than Carmen begins trying to persuade José to let her escape. She engages him in conversation concerning his home region Navarre (which we already know to be his weak spot); and even though he unmasks her claim that she too is from Navarre, he remains gullible throughout the exchange. Recognizing his vulnerability, José orders her to cease speaking, and once again she resorts to performing a song. If José has yet to utter

Ex. 9

Près   des rem - parts   de Sé - vil - - -

- le,   Chez— mon a - mi— Lil - las

Pas - tia

a note except in the secure context of his encounter with Micaëla, Carmen has yet to sing anything other than a pop tune.

Seguidilla and Duet (B minor)

Like the song Carmen sang during the exchange with Zuniga, the "Seguidilla" is designed to suggest flamenco dance (Ex. 9). It is strongly physical and features modal ambiguities that make the song slippery, difficult to define tonally. At times it seems securely in F♯ major, then in D major, finally in B minor. In the middle section, as she both offers and withholds herself, her chromatic treachery becomes almost intolerable as the points of tonal reference in both bass and melody wriggle about by contrary-motion half-steps. And when she returns to her opening materials, it is by mere fiat as she simply wills herself back to F♯/B minor.

No wonder, then, that José can bear it no longer. He reminds her that he has forbidden her to speak to him. But he does so in recitative, even in Bizet's version. None of her previous provocations had succeeded in making him let down his guard: he has always maintained either silence or speech in her presence. His spontaneous eruption into sung declamation here signals his defeat. She replies quietly that she is not speaking, but only singing; moreover, she insists that she is not addressing him, but sings for her own pleasure. These are the two crucial distinctions José never grasps: that she may be performing rather than interacting and that he may be irrelevant to her utterances rather than their intended target. Narcissistic bourgeois subject that he most fatally is, he believes in the transparency of language and in himself as the perspectival center of his universe. He thus has no defenses against

Ex. 10

this woman who is a virtuoso of irony, ambiguity, slippage, decentering and multiple discursive practices.

She pivots to Db major to sing of a "certain officer" who loves her and whom she might well love in return. And here she plays her trump card. For while she is not herself a member of José's dominant class, she has (as an alien living under the control of this group) learned how to wield its codes like a native speaker. Thus as she begins to sing of love, she pivots into the mode of lyric urgency that marked José's and Micaëla's interchanges (Ex. 10). If he managed to hold back from the corrupt currency of her "gypsy" songs, José swallows this simulacrum of "authenticity" hook, line and sinker. When she pulls back to her song (still in the remote flat keys), he clamors to respond to her. He repeats her bait, a pitch higher; and while Carmen had presented her cadence through understatement, José heroically caps off his reply with a climactic a♯ [1]. The "Seguidilla" rhythms return as he tries to force promises from her while acquiescing in her escape: musically, he holds on to his monotonal b♮ for dear life, while Carmen slides about chromatically, always just out of reach. She finally responds by singing once more the refrain of her song, which is as much answer as José is granted.

Finale (F minor; D♭ major; A major)

When Zuniga reappears, the women's fighting chorus is heard as a fugue in the strings, now in F minor rather than F♯. The formal certainty of earlier scenes has become increasingly shaky. As José begins to lead Carmen away, she stops to taunt Zuniga with the "Habañera" refrain, now in D♭, rather than D major. Her accompaniment is strangely still: she sings over sustained strings in what sounds like suspended animation. The orchestral postlude becomes treacherous as d♭ becomes c♯ and the tonality wavers. Suddenly, Carmen shoves José and escapes, with the music of the fighting chorus (now in A major) and their laughter resounding triumphantly.

Like scene v, this finale is a grab-bag which wraps up some loose ends and attenuates others. In some sense, the last four scenes (beginning with the women's fighting chorus) form a unit that here reaches closure – at least thematically. But while the impression of symmetrical return prevails at the conclusion of this first act, the question of *whose* symmetry is still open, perhaps more than ever. Tonally, we have returned to the key signature of three sharps (F♯ minor/A major) that opened scene vii; but since the relative major usually does not stand for adequate closure, this triumphant ending seems somewhat false. Yet we began the entire opera with a prelude that opened in A major, so it may be that we are being given thematic recall from one terrain and tonal return from another.

In both cases, we have the triumph of what has been marked as Other: the female factory workers, Carmen and the Spanish exoticism of the prelude. The *boulevardiers* of the opening segments and Don José have been drawn into a world in which they thought they were merely observing these "odd people." By the end of Act I, they have been overwhelmed by those very Others who seem now to control the frame.

Entr'acte (G minor/G major)

This is the first of three entr'actes: orchestral interludes that either set the atmosphere for the beginning of the following scene or – as with this one – introduce materials that are later thematized dramatically. In terms of dramaturgical strategy, they help draw the audience back from intermission into a receptive, attentive mood before the action recommences. This first entr'acte turns out to be the soldier's watch song sung by Don José later in the act as he approaches Lillas Pastia's; accordingly it has qualities of the military and also José's solitude or alienation. But as it first appears, it gives Bizet the opportunity to display his craft at manipulating orchestral colors, motives and affect outside the pressures of the drama.

Act II

Gypsy Song (E minor)

The act opens in Lillas Pastia's establishment – the place Carmen designated in the "Seguidilla" as her favorite rendezvous. It is in this scene that Carmen appears most explicitly as an entertainer, rather than as a character who may or may not be revealing "authentic" truths about herself. Indeed, the lyrics she sings boast of her methods as a performer and the desired effects of her exotic gypsy music and dance: its ability to arouse sensual passion, frenzy, inebriation – the very symptoms José has begun to manifest. Because this set-piece represents an actual song-and-dance number within the opera, it can afford to be extravagant in its staging. It offers us a full-blown cabaret spectacle in the context of our bourgeois *opéra-comique*.

Bizet's style during this scene resembles Spanish music perhaps more closely than any of his other exotic numbers (see Chapter 4). In its sultry introduction, it adopts the descending tetrachord progression often associated with flamenco music. As was the case in previous exotic numbers (the prelude, the "Seguidilla"), this number is marked by flashy orchestration, frank sensuality and erratic shifts in harmonic orientation for the sake of color. As in the "Habañera," Carmen here sings a strophic song with major-mode choral refrains, and again she sings chromatic descents over a static bass. The style of this piece suggests all the more that the

"Habañera" was likewise a standard cabaret number. As the women perform, they simulate the frenzied passion they purport to be inspiring by accelerating and finally opening out into an orgiastic orchestral postlude, now scarcely recognizable as the same tetrachord descent that opened the scene. But whereas a flamenco progression of this sort defines the lowest pitch of the tetrachord as the goal of the progression, the tonal ear hears that pitch as having a dominant function; and Bizet seals the scene up by having the progression resolve dutifully back to what he and his audience would have perceived as tonic: the pitch that initiated the descent, E.

In the ensuing dialogue, Lillas Pastia declares that it is closing-time and tries to evict the soldiers who are present. Zuniga mutters about the actual purpose of this establishment and attempts to persuade the women (Carmen especially) to go with him. Carmen learns that José has spent a month in prison for having helped her escape and that he has just been released, stripped of his status as officer. Zuniga notices that her mood improves with this news, and her response – an aside, "Et j'ai raison" – is one of the few indications we have that she has any regard for José at all. Even this fragment is ambiguous: it could reflect her confidence in her ability to attract men. It scarcely proves that she has pined for him in the intervening month.

Chorus and Ensemble (C major)

A march and triumphal chorus is heard offstage, over which the spoken dialogue continues, though now focused on the event transpiring outside. The famous torero Escamillo and his fans are passing by, and Zuniga and the others invite him in. It is thus that José's rival makes his entrance: in contrast to José's first appearance, Escamillo's advent is heralded with fanfares and public acclamation, rather than with piccolos and children pretending to be soldiers. The 6/8 meter of his entry only accentuates the swaggering machismo that always characterizes Escamillo, again in counterdistinction to José's bourgeois sentiment and naïvely earnest passion.

Couplet: "Toreador Song" (F minor/F major)

No less than Carmen, Escamillo is a charismatic performer. And in this – his signature number – he displays himself for his adoring public, describing as self-reflexively as did Carmen in her gypsy song his skill at manipulating audiences in the arena. Escamillo and Carmen are a matched pair: both belong to the gaudy world of mass entertainment, and although both are experts at simulating affect and arousing it in others, neither of them betrays emotions readily or unambiguously. This may be because they are shallow, hard, devoid of interiority (unlike their bourgeois counterparts); or it may be that they are in greater control of their feelings and thus are in a better position to manipulate others. However one reads them, they represent threats to the world of bourgeois "sincerity" in which character and feelings are transparent. But they also locate and play upon important lacks in that bourgeois world: a world that denies the body, that can deal with sexuality only if it is disguised as maternal affection and filial duty.

Like Carmen's music, Escamillo's is strongly physical, although his rhythms suggest not dance but the flamboyant gestures of the bullfights. His characteristic pattern alternates between percussive motives and suspense, and the orchestra lavishes his every move with ornaments. As he describes the blow-by-blow action of the bullring, he remains in the minor mode with mock-dangerous Neapolitan inflections; but as he turns to the matter of the woman who awaits his victory, he pivots to the major and the simulation of tenderness. The march we heard in the prelude returns, now firmly tied to Escamillo – to his prowess as torero and lover (Bizet asks that this be sung "fatuously"). As is also the case with Carmen's production numbers, the chorus enters to reflect his glory, as it repeats and amplifies his statements. His identity too is socially grounded and celebrated. Moreover, he forms a constituent part of the framing complex: his music (not José's) was announced during the prelude itself.

At the conclusion of the second strophe, the gypsy women disrupt closure by taking the word "l'amour" and playing with it suggestively, to which Escamillo answers in kind. Finally, Carmen seizes the word and destabilizes it: she sings in a lower register and with risky intervals, ending with an augmented octave. This too Escamillo answers, but with a certainty that seals an intimate understanding between them alone. The chorus bursts in and brings the number to a decisive close. A dialogue ensues in which Escamillo tests Carmen's availability. She encourages his attentions while remaining aloof. Zuniga asks Carmen if he may return to see her later, which she advises him not to do. He leaves with Escamillo's party.

Chorus (E major)

Escamillo and his entourage exit with a reprise of the "Toreador Song," transposed now down a half-step. Its earlier brilliance is now but reminiscence. Gradually the number trails off into fragments and a pizzicato cadence. Like the first act, the initial scenes in Act II reach easy closure, and nothing seems to challenge its formal plan. But the world revealed thus far in this act is the world of the indigenous population: if the disruptive element in the first act was Carmen, this act unfolds untroubled on her turf.

When Escamillo and Zuniga have departed, the gypsies begin the deliberations delayed by the torero's appearance. For the gypsies – when they are not providing exotic entertainment for the sake of the mainstream population – are smugglers, and they are eager to arrange a plan of action. Meilhac's comic touch is most apparent in these gypsy dialogues, in the exchanges between the "boss" El Dancaïre and the servile El Remendado. In Mérimée, Carmen herself often leads the gang; in the opera, she operates under male leadership – even the gypsies have been rendered patriarchal. Guiraud's version eliminates most of Meilhac's dialogue altogether.

Quintet (Db major)

The smugglers develop their plans during a quintet sung by the two men, along with Mercédès, Frasquita and Carmen. As the men inform the women of their responsibilities during this job, the tone is hushed, rapid-fire, conspiratorial. The men and women banter back and forth during their negotiations, displaying relative equality: when the gypsies get down to work, everyone participates. Still, the division of labor is gendered, for the lyrics insist that in matters of trickery, women are more effective than men. Such a sentiment cuts both ways: within the context of this den of thieves, such qualities are esteemed as signs of professional competence; but within the context of the opera, the lyrics serve to underscore Woman's essential treachery.

Like the numbers in the first half of Act I, the quintet is constructed through nested symmetries. The opening material returns after a short contrasting section in the minor, and the whole quintet-complex returns for formal closure at the end of the scene. Enclosed in the middle of the scene is a sequence in which Carmen announces that she does not intend to come along because she is "in love." The others scoff, and Carmen herself exhibits considerable self-parody with respect to her "love-stricken" state: she uses exaggerated gestures to convey her sentiments and echoes their teasing passage concerning "love and duty." Yet she remains firm in her decision, and the beginning of the quintet returns to close out the scene. Her resistance does not threaten this social order: her whims are too well known to be taken seriously, and she remains securely within the community. In the dialogue that follows, Carmen confesses that she awaits José. They bet he will fail to show up; but just as Carmen announces her confidence, José is heard singing in the distance as he approaches.

Song (G minor/G major)

José now makes his second entrance. Unlike his regiment or Escamillo, he is unheralded except by his own unaccompanied singing. He performs the march we heard earlier as entr'acte, before we entered the gypsy world. While his lyrics indicate that he too is singing a preexistent song (a watchman's dialogue with a dragoon of Alcala), they strike a couple of significant thematic chords: the dragoon returns to avenge himself on his rival (as José will do repeatedly), and he insists on honor in matters of the heart. If he is ostensibly singing to himself, he also signals to Carmen – if unwittingly – his deadly intentions. He sings the song through twice. Between renditions, Carmen discusses with the gypsies her attraction: José is pretty, he pleases her. Her colleagues know her well enough to see him as a passing fancy: she will soon rejoin the fold.

During the ensuing dialogue between Carmen and José, we learn that Carmen had sent him a file to help him escape from prison but that he used it only to sharpen his lance: the tool intended for freedom became the means of refining a weapon. Carmen tells him he missed her performance, and the news that she dances publicly arouses his ire. She flirts and draws a confession of love from him (a word that means something very different in the mouths of Carmen, Escamillo and the gypsies). And she reveals in quick succession a few other dimensions of her character. First, she abides by the gypsy law that requires the paying of debts: José went to prison after they made their pact in the opening act, and she is prepared to uphold her end of the bargain by dancing and drinking with him (her only pledge: "J'irai danser la Séguedille et boire du Manzanilla"). Second, she is greedy: José remarks that she gobbles down bonbons like a child; she is, we know, this way with men as well. Third, she is resourceful yet destructive: when she fails to locate her castanets, she casually shatters a dish and uses its fragments for her accompaniment. At this point in the drama, virtually every line from either Carmen or José is laden with portent. Finally, Carmen offers to dance for José alone.

> *Duet* (Bb major; G major/minor; Db major; C major/minor)

This complex number perplexed the first performers and audiences because of its radical continuity. Since the scene is responsible for establishing the unorthodox dynamics of the Carmen/José relationship, it necessarily refuses division into the tidy numbers that usually ordered *opéra-comique* and even (up until this point) this particular work.

Carmen begins by performing another song-and-dance number. This one resembles the others only in that its rhythmic impulse is strongly physical: her usual chromaticism and modal ambiguity are gone, replaced here by a diatonic tune harmonized by predictable tonic and dominant alternations. There are at least two reasons for this change in Carmen's discourse. First, her tune is to be combined with a military bugle call, and it must be able to occupy the same tonal space. But before this superimposition occurs, Carmen's song has to make sense in its own right, and her diatonicism indicates a straightforwardness absent from her previous songs. For all her earlier, public numbers were designed to arouse, tease and yet withhold. If she still foregrounds her body in her song for José, it is because she is offering it to him in an intimate encounter. There are no chromatic tricks, no modal ambivalences here.

As was the case with her "Tra la la" refrain of Act I, Carmen here dispenses with words. Her seduction is sensual rather than verbal, which makes it more treacherous (José's bourgeois universe depends on verbal intentions, and the nonverbal media of dance and song influence him more powerfully than words) and more evasive (it is not clear what this song means or even *that* it means, enhancing Carmen's inscrutability). Suddenly the bugles play the call to duty, ironically harmonizing perfectly with Carmen's song of sensual delight. José interrupts Carmen, drawing her attention to the bugles. She playfully appropriates the military signal as her accompaniment and continues to dance. Another of José's marches is subverted: what he salutes as a symbol of honor is converted (like the shattered dish) into a mere accompaniment for Carmen's pleasure. Again he interrupts her: he must return obediently to his quarters.

Carmen is not amused. She unleashes a whole range of vituperations (self-mockery, sarcasm, insults, rage) that José doubtless has never heard issuing from a woman. Her phrases are short, aggressive, unpredictable in their onslaught; they build to her demand (punctuated with a decisive cadence on G major) that he return to camp. José enters, whining that her abuse is unjust, that he loves her more than any other woman. He pivots into a pathetic G minor, but soon maneuvers through a deceptive cadence into the fantasy key of the sixth degree, Eb major.

The sentimental arpeggios that underpinned and propeled his interchanges with Micaëla reappear: we are suddenly in the realm of bourgeois accompaniments and "authentic" expression – what Dahlhaus characterizes as José's "lyric urgency." As is his custom when displaying sincere emotions, José here creates a pitch ceiling, then pushes it up bit by bit until he seems to transcend the obstacle heroically. He begins with a depressed cb, alters it sequentially upward to d^1, f^1 and finally a♮^{1}, harmonized in brilliant C major. After this climactic moment, he guides his phrase back to the Eb major he had so tenuously established as his point of departure. He enacts in his music a standard vision of bourgeois teleology in which melodic sequences and subtle harmonic shifts grant the illusion of ultimate goals successfully attained.

But his romantic outburst fails to address the matter at hand, verbally or musically. Carmen punctures his balloon by reharmonizing his Eb goal with B major and repeating her sarcastic depiction of him running back to camp. Again José responds with pathos – G minor and viola figuration representing his surging emotions. This time, instead of escaping to his dream world, he remains aware of Carmen, insisting – despite her resistance – that she listen to him ("Tu m'entendras!"). In the silence that follows his demand (marked "violently"), he draws from his tunic the flower Carmen had hurled at him, and the prelude/Carmen motive appears (see Ex. 3) – in the sultry English horn. The motivic sequence twists around to a pedal on Bb and from there to Db major for José's celebrated monologue, "Flower Song."

Note that this key of Db has been established only by multiple tenuous means: the place from which José launches his most sustained appeal has no base in reality. Indeed, it is even more of a pipe dream than his previous sixth-degree excursion. Accordingly, he sets out tentatively, with halting syncopations in the accompaniment. He takes few chances in the first segment but holds tight to diatonic progressions that return him safely to the tonic. Having successfully negotiated his opening gambit, José becomes more reckless: as he recalls sniffing the flower in prison, he pivots enharmonically into remote key areas. But with his climactic ab^1 ("je m'enivrais" – "I became intoxicated") he seizes the key of Db once again and anchors the second segment of his speech in Carmen's image. As in the prelude, Bizet here pulls us into a game of "fort-da," in which ever greater risks are undertaken with the assumption that one can always return. Such formal assumptions prove unreliable in *Carmen*.

Suddenly José modulates from serenity to hate, marked harmonically by a move to Bb minor – the relative minor of Db. But then he repents his slander and glides into his most sustained climactic sequence. As his arpeggios finally appear, he starts to ascend by step. To accommodate his melodic climb, the harmonies twist around erratically: F major, D major, Bb major – each standing in the position of sixth degree to the preceding center – and then down by step to F. Over this last progression and the text "un seul désir, un seul espoir," a ceiling is set up creating the impression of frustration as he sticks on f^1, apparently incapable of pushing beyond. Finally, he reaches climax, again by calling out explicitly for Carmen, and this brings him back to Db major. The challenges were far more serious this time around, and the need for force seemed inherent within the tendencies of the pitches themselves.

Now the arpeggios increase in urgency as José holds triumphantly to the Db tonality he has conquered. Over a Db pedal, he begins to sequence downward, gradually dissipating the effect of his climax as he explains how Carmen has possessed his being. But as he sings masochistically of how he has delivered himself over to her as her object ("Et j'étais une chose à toi"), he mounts stepwise without accompaniment to a high bb^1, the climax of the entire song. This pitch is highly vulnerable – it is marked pianissimo; and as sixth-degree, it exceeds the control of the tonic triad. Yet it is harmonized with a hymn-like subdominant (one imagines it returning to tonic as a prolonged "Amen"); the certainty he has sought throughout the song seems all but granted. His line has but to ascend stepwise back to tonic for closure.

On the penultimate pitch, however – the leading tone c^1 – the winds enter with a series of harmonizations that imply everything but the expected dominant of D♭. The moment that most reliably grants the illusion of cause and effect in tonal music is thereby undermined. Much depends on how one interprets those chords: do they represent José's subjectivity, straining to invest even this cliché with heartfelt significance? Or are they indications that his assertion of certainty is nothing more than that: an assertion of faith in the face of grave doubt?

Whatever they mean, the D♭ tonic appears at the end, and all is well. But Carmen prevents the applause that ought to have erupted at this moment with a deft tritone move to g^1. After José's glorious enactment of passion, she merely mutters "Non! tu ne m'aimes pas" ("No, you don't love me"). In a sense, she is right. She is but a pretext for José's fantasies. At the moment when she expects interaction, he sings to her of his fantasies in prison as evidence of his devotion. Moreover, Carmen and José have revealed themselves to have two very different models of sexual pleasure: Carmen's is firmly grounded in sensuality and the body, while José's attempts to transcend the body through violent striving, conquests, climaxes. Hers involves opening up to another human being; his demands single-minded control and possession.

Immediately Carmen replaces José's image of violent passion with her own solution: that he leave with her and the smugglers to enjoy liberty outside the law. As usual, her music is highly rhythmic – a rolling 6/8 in C major; it is a fully formed set-piece that might be a preexistent song in celebration of gypsy life. José protests impotently a couple of times with the appoggiatura figures that express longing, but Carmen gallops on, pulling José unwillingly into her plan as she did at the conclusion of Act I. He finally breaks in with a last-ditch effort at extricating himself. Again he appeals to honor, to her pity, and then makes his melodramatic leave with impassioned high notes and a definitive cadence in C minor. As he approaches the door, the orchestra thunders out a motive that resembles Carmen's motive, but it appears here in diatonic transformation, as though he and normative tonality have wrested themselves free of her chromatic inflections. But his exit is blocked by an abrupt diminished seventh.

Finale (F♯ minor; A major; C major)

Zuniga returns, hoping for Carmen's favors. He enters, assesses the situation and orders José back to camp. José draws his saber, and the two must be separated by the gypsies. Once Zuniga is disarmed, Carmen and the gypsies make fun of his predicament with mock-galantries, to which he responds ironically in kind. But now that José has committed a direct act of insubordination, it is no longer possible for him to return to the army. Carmen repeats her song in praise of gypsy life, and the others join her for a spirited finale.

This act ends like the one before, with Carmen successfully engineering an escape as José sinks further into despair and degradation. These parallel endings occur even though in some important sense the structures of the acts were inversions of one another: in the first act, the soldiers set the context, which Carmen destabilized; in the second, the gypsies established the mood, and José destabilized it. But destabilization in both situations culminates in José's defeat, while Carmen wins in both contexts. And both endings are marked musically as triumphs rather than tragedy. It is as though she controls the crucial affective moments, and we retreat to the lobby in a celebratory mood, even though our protagonist is in dire straits.

Entr'acte (E♭ major)

Like the previous entr'acte, the one that opens the third act both prepares the scene that follows and also pulls back from the frenzy of the preceding act. José has fled with Carmen to the countryside, and the entr'acte paints this landscape with the conventional signs of pastorale. The major-mode harmonies are static (at least initially), and while the harp arpeggiates, the flute plays a serene, freely arching melody. Other instruments enter to converse imitatively with the flute, enhancing the entr'acte's utopian quality. In terms of the distinctions upon which this opera relies, this music belongs to the terrain of José and Micaëla. True to type, it becomes agitated in the middle and moves sequentially to a passionate climax before restoring the calm opening materials. The movement ends softly with the median pitch high in the flute.

While this charming entr'acte provides a moment of respite, it is deceptively calming. Towards the middle, the curtain rises to reveal anything but the domesticated setting of the conventional pastorale. It is night, and we are shown a wild, savage landscape marked with craggy rocks and utter solitude. Once again a fissure opens up between romantic, bourgeois ideals (those shared by the audience and their stand-in, José) and stark reality.

Act III

Introduction (C minor)

The next music we hear suits this wilderness far better. As the smugglers make their way down the rocks under heavy burdens, the orchestra plays a furtive march. The elements of flute and strings remain constant from the entr'acte (we are still in a rural setting), but now they conform to the exigencies of plot and landscape. Repeatedly the melody progresses to Eb major, only to return to C minor at the beginning of the next phrase, as though each step forward is but part of the endless drudgery of the smugglers' labor.

The chorus of gypsy smugglers comes in only in the march's contrasting "trio" section. They sing over an Ab major pedal – the sixth degree that hangs precariously above the dominant of C minor; while it seems more stable and optimistic, less oppressive than the opening, it is a very treacherous toehold. The gypsies warn each other to be careful, but still are pulled back to the return of the beginning. They dramatize this backsliding ("Prends garde de faire un faux pas!") by descending chromatically, with tortured harmonies that return inexorably to C minor.

The chorus unfolds through nested symmetries, as have earlier opening scenes: this too is a self-contained world. As in previous choruses, we get a strong sense of community in this number as the gypsies articulate the virtue of their outlaw existence, its superiority to that of the soldier who stands guard against them. This is the opposite viewpoint from that expressed by the soldiers in Act I. In this opera, it is the gypsies who exhibit industry and camaraderie, while the soldiers (those invested with official power) are but girl-watching loiterers, eager to fight each other when competing for Carmen's favors. We witness the decadence of the bourgeoisie and the threat of a well-organized network of guerrillas and criminals.

In the ensuing dialogue, the smugglers discuss plans; then Carmen and José enter. They have quarreled, and José wants to reconcile. Carmen admits that she loves him less, that she may cease to love him altogether. When José recalls his mother, Carmen suggests that he return home. He responds with a veiled threat, and she realizes that he would kill her before letting her go. He calls her a devil, a designation she gladly accepts if it will persuade him to leave. Their relationship has soured, has run aground on its own contradictions. As Carmen mentions, she has already foreseen in the cards that they would meet their ends together. She is resigned to this fate and does nothing to stave it off: she will remain true to herself to death.

Trio (A minor/F major)

Carmen's companions, Frasquita and Mercédès, begin to shuffle cards to tell their fortunes. Their duet alternates between mock-portentousness (in A minor) and a refrain (F major) that reveals it all to be a girlish game. Each tells her own future – made up of stock romantic clichés that provoke their laughter – then returns to the refrain.

Carmen decides to try her luck. The tonality moves back towards minor for her entry, which occurs over ominous open fifths. As she turns up her cards, the flirtatious motive from her Act I entrance sounds, but its ironic quality is destroyed by a sudden chromatic sweep as she finds death (hers and José's). She breaks off her prophecy with "La mort!" – which resonates with her earlier refrain "L'amour" – and on a tenuous db^1 that pivots into sombre F minor. At this point, Carmen sings her only number in the opera that is not primarily a song for public performance. She muses on the meaning of the cards, her faith in their accuracy and her belief that death with José inevitably awaits her. Interestingly, here where we presumably overhear her private thoughts for the first time, she sings not in the style of her characteristic gypsy discourse, but rather in the tongue of "universal" subjectivity. As she faces death, she is no longer radically Other; she is just like everyone else – i.e., just like José and his audience.

Carmen sings with a halting, stagnant accompaniment that resembles a funeral dirge. Yet her melody roams free as she courageously confronts her fate. She seeks refuge temporarily in what she herself marks as the falseness of Ab major, and then leads back sequentially (over an inexorable rising bass) to a climactic return of F minor, which she embraces. In this lament, her *modus operandi* is José's, except that she avoids his violence. Still, while this is her only intimate utterance in the opera, it too is strangely impersonal. For she sings not about her own feelings so much as about the cards, fate and one's inability to alter their predictions. Yet if she resigns herself to fate, it is because she has faith in such portents – not because of love for José, which is extinguished. As she approaches her dark final pitch, the merry refrain of her companions breaks in to complete the number. Even Carmen's prophecy of death can be contained, though the refrain's gaiety turns ironic with her foreboding interventions. And despite two brief occurrences of Carmen's motive, the number ends securely in F major.

In the dialogue that follows, the gypsies learn that three customs agents guard the place they had hoped to enter. Over José's objections, Carmen volunteers her services and those of the other women: they will go and distract the agents so that the band can get through.

Ensemble (Gb major)

Carmen and her companions launch into a swaggering march in which they boast of their talents in distracting enemies. The strategies they describe resemble only too closely the situation in Act I, in which Carmen seduced José. The currency José took to be authentic may never have been anything but the trick of a gypsy who regards sexual favors and affections as resources in espionage. The chorus joins in celebrating the women's skill and the stupidity of pleasure-loving officials who are so readily tricked. The middle section becomes slippery with Carmen's favorite devices – chromaticism, enharmonic pivots – as she and others describe their treachery. The chorus concludes with utter confidence, for these moments of slippage, far from endangering formal containment, are actually the means by which the gypsies maintain control.

The intruder in this act is Micaëla, entering with a guide who has led her to José's band. We learn that she intends to confront the gypsies alone. The guide wishes her divine protection and leaves. The recitative version eliminates the guide, and Micaëla unaccountably wanders on to the scene by herself. Guiraud's background music during this passage resembles Weber's Wolf Glen, with its mysterious diminished-seventh tremolos, afterbeats, and even a heroic outburst that seems patterned after Agatha's heroic leitmotiv. Although Bizet's version employs only spoken dialogue in this section, he has already made use of Weber's vocabulary of ultimate evil throughout the opera, always associated with Carmen. Guiraud may draw rather too obviously on *Der Freischütz* here, but Bizet has prepared the way. Indeed, the dramatic function of the ensuing air recalls Agatha's "Leise, leise" in *Der Freischütz*: both are prayers of pure young women striving to ward off evil and to redeem the endangered loved one.

Air (E♭ major)

Gounod claimed that this air (in his estimation, the only melody in *Carmen* of any worth) was his. Whether or not this is so, this air is one of the few passages in Bizet's opera that sound like conventional *opéra-comique*. This is no accident – Micaëla was introduced into the libretto specifically to appeal to the bourgeois audience and serve as a foil to Carmen, which she does during the remainder of this act. During her air, Micaëla reveals herself to be heroic and – while frightened – confident in her faith. She is capable of creating rounded structures, of overcoming doubt with certainty. The general effect of the principal part of the air is that of calm – the static harmonies, arpeggiated figuration and serenely undulating melody identify her as a creature of the entr'acte's pastoral countryside. Yet there are periodic disturbances as she reflects upon her mission: in the first phrase, her melody rises anxiously up through f♯^{2} to g^2 before she exercises self-control and brings it back down into her confident middle range. Later, as she reflects on the wildness of the surrounding landscape, she seems to become trapped in an oppressive G minor. But drawing upon her faith and passion, she manages to break through into the light of C major and thence to an elaborate return to E♭.

The middle section of the air concerns her anticipated meeting with Carmen, whom she suspects of having seduced José through witchcraft ("artifices maudits"). She calls for God's protection against this dangerous, beautiful, heathen woman. While imagining Carmen and their confrontation, Micaëla braves the slippery chromatic terrain associated with Carmen. Each moment of the fantasy pulls her into dangerous minor-mode regions, which she always successfully negotiates, even when it leads her to an impassioned climax on b♮^{2}, a pitch quite alien to her tonic E♭. The climax leads to a secure cadence in G major, which pivots back easily through the common-tone g^1 to Eb and the return of the opening material.

Unlike José, whose tonal and formal worlds are fatally destabilized by Carmen's presence, Micaëla can pass through these waters unsullied. Her purity, Christianity and harmonic pedals serve as talismans to ward off evil. Her air concludes simply, confidently with a cause-effect melodic resolution up to eb^2, harmonically endorsed by a dominant seventh resolving to tonic. By contrast, José's attempt at resolving the leading tone back to tonic at the end of his "Flower Song" was harmonically shaky, riddled with doubt. Following the conclusion of her superbly self-contained air, Micaëla spots Don José and calls to him. A shot is fired. She hides as Escamillo enters and introduces himself to José.

Duet (F major)

The first section of the duet presents exchanges between Escamillo and José in accompanied recitative. Escamillo is initially welcomed as a celebrity, but as he explains his mission – that he seeks his lover – José begins to suspect their rivalry. At last Escamillo identifies his "gypsy girl" (whom he marks with the augmented second that suggests "Oriental" and sensuality): she is Carmen. He sings about his love in Db, but as José pushes him to name her, he veers back to F minor. The fatal name "Carmen" echoes between the men, solidifying the cadence.

Escamillo returns to Db to recount as a rumor the failed affair between Carmen and José. This key and Escamillo's accompaniment recall the "Flower Song": everyone knows José's shame, even his mode of expression. When Escamillo observes that Carmen's loves are fleeting, José responds with disbelief: how, knowing this, can Escamillo love Carmen? Escamillo replies with an extravagant affirmation of his love. José announces that those who would take away gypsy women must fight to the death. Escamillo at last recognizes José. He taunts José with a chromatic descent reminiscent of the "Habañera" that first snagged José. Together they launch into a blustering duet in which each sings of his motives for fighting while warning the other to beware. The number ends with an F major postlude during which they duel.[4] The postlude halts abruptly on a diminished seventh as Escamillo's weapon breaks and José lunges to kill him.

Finale (F major)

The concluding number to Act III takes every dramatic strand in the opera and intensifies it, making clear the impossibility of a nonviolent solution. Carmen interrupts José as he prepares to murder Escamillo, and Escamillo gallantly thanks her for saving his life. He challenges José to renew their combat at a future date and announces his next bullfight. He issues a special invitation to Carmen ("Et qui m'aime y viendra!"). Suddenly, he shifts gear to a stern march, the bass line of which teeters ominously between E and Ab major as he casts one more warning to José and says his farewells. He exits in Db to a somewhat dreamy rendition (cellos *divisi*) of his signature "Toreador Song." José lunges again, only to be restrained by the gypsies. He threatens Carmen, but is interrupted by El Dancaïro's order that they break camp.

Preparations break off suddenly as Micaëla is discovered hiding. In response to José's demands that she explain her presence, she offers up a series of reminiscences from Act I, reminding José and the audience how far he has fallen since that innocent encounter. She begins to sing a line in A minor, stops, then pivots into the sentimental Bb passage that had previously proved so effective with José (see Ex. 8). As before, this melody accompanies her description of José's mother, who now grieves for him. Micaëla pleads with him to return.

Carmen tells José to leave: he never belonged anyway. He responds with an agitated air that swings wildly among a variety of keys before settling on a resolute sequential line in the extreme key of Gb major ("Dût-il m'en coûter la vie") in which he vows to hold on to Carmen if it costs him his life. The gypsies interject that it may cost him his life if he doesn't leave. A struggle ensues; José erupts once again with his "Dût-il" refrain (now in G major), cursing Carmen and their entangled fates. As the gypsies again warn him, Micaëla tells him (with the melody she could not complete at the beginning of the scene) that his mother is dying. José agrees to go with her, but only after insisting that he and Carmen will meet again. His cadence is greeted by a snarling presentation of the prelude's "fate" materials, which suddenly melt into F major as Escamillo sings his signature tune offstage. Carmen moves to follow him, but José menacingly blocks her path. As the curtain falls, the gypsies take up their burdens and depart. The orchestra plays a placid, F major version of the smugglers' march that opened the act.

At the close of Act III, the gypsy world remains intact – the act begins and ends with their nomadic music. Likewise, Escamillo and Micaëla have both reappeared, their identities securely grounded in their respective themes. As Carmen claims, however, José has no place in this world, and his erratic behavior has become intolerably dissonant. He leaves, temporarily purging the scene of his violence. But his threats hang over the conclusion of the act in the db-c dissenting appoggiaturas that mar the otherwise affirmative cadence. His return is inevitable.

Entr'acte (A phrygian/D minor)

The exotic, flashy pseudo-gypsy music of Act II returns. Again Bizet suggests flamenco music through modal inflections, guitar-like vamps, sharp rhythmic punctuations, exotic percussion, sinuous chromaticism and descending tetrachords. At the end, he gives the main tune a decisively tonal harmonization to secure it. The concluding major triad may be heard as dominant of D minor or a picardy alteration of the phrygian tonic. In either case, the slippery ambiguities of the entr'acte are mollified by this affirmative sonority.

Act IV

Chorus (G major)

Like the beginning of Act I, the final act opens in daylight. We return to a public space where people assemble for a festival and street vendors sell oranges and cigarettes. Constant eighth notes in the accompaniment provide a sense of excitement. During a brief contrasting section, Zuniga (always angling for women) buys oranges for a young girl, but they are soon reabsorbed by the crowd and its music. The scene reestablishes a kind of communal normalcy, temporarily dispelling the dark, claustrophobic settings of Acts II and III. At the number's close, Zuniga and Carmen's friends exchange news: Carmen is with Escamillo and José has disappeared from his village, where soldiers had gone to arrest him. Frasquita fears for Carmen's safety.

Chorus and Scene (A major)

As the toreros enter, the crowd celebrates. The chorus builds over a pedal to the emergence of the prelude's opening segment, in its original key: thus this tune too belongs to Escamillo. Its return resembles the return of the overture in *Don Giovanni*, at which point the opera's frame closes in fatefully. But if Mozart's theme portended tragedy, this one is exceedingly cheerful. It is as though José has simply evaporated, leaving the terrain to gypsies and bullfighters.

As in the prelude, this scene follows a symmetrical process in which contrasting materials alternate with the refrain. This time there is an extra insertion (in D major), in which the crowd describes the toreros as they march by. A second insertion in F major remains in that key for the refrain, rather than returning to A major. As the crowd recognizes Escamillo, the tonality destabilizes, only to lead back with their acclamations not to the refrain (which we are led to expect), but to the "Toreador Song" – now in A rather than its usual F major. Escamillo seems to have captured the tonality of the opera. His theme is in consonant solidarity with the celebratory music of the beginning, which returns to embrace his entrance.

Escamillo turns to Carmen, and they sing a touchingly simple exchange in which they publicly declare their love for one another. Escamillo sings in D major, Carmen responds with the same music in G. Next both sing together ("Ah! je t'aime") in unison, then in sweet parallel sixths as they round off their duet in D. Bizet never presents such unanimity of feeling between Carmen and José. They sing the same music only when Carmen mocks José or tricks him into thinking they speak the same tongue, as in the "Seguidilla." The Escamillo/Carmen duet is sometimes criticized as a cliché, in contrast to the complex, passionate relationship between José and Carmen. But this brief exchange can be heard as revealing those qualities the affair with José lacks: tenderness, mutual trust, equality. José's inability to envision love along these lines fuels his violence, his need for domination that leads finally to Carmen's murder.

A short episode in Eb major plays as the crowd enters the arena. While the music remains frivolous and gay, it forms the backdrop over which Carmen's friends warn her of José's presence. Carmen says that she will meet him. They are apprehensive, but she insists.

The music accelerates and leads back to A major and opening prelude materials that have organized this entire number. This would seem to secure closure; but as José appears, the fissures between phrases are filled by ominous, chromatically-descending octaves. Carmen's flirtation motive enters quietly, answered by a chromatic bass that dissolves into a maddeningly slippery floor, pushing us forward into the final scene. The effect resembles the abrupt end of the prelude, which likewise dumps us out into a void. This time, however, the issue will not be sidestepped. It will continue to its "natural" conclusion.

> *Duet-Finale* (a variety of shifting key centers, culminating in F♯ major)

In this final number, we are pulled down into the vortex of José's frustrated passion. As has been the case with every encounter between the two leads, this finale struggles between the plot's unpredictable eruptions and the music's demand for formal symmetry. José attempts to impose a trajectory of "lyric urgency": his conviction that he can persuade Carmen to give herself over to him creates the maniacal thrust that compels us forward. By contrast, Carmen speaks plainly; she tries to explain her reasons for leaving him, tries to defuse his murderous rage. Overarching the entire scene is the prelude-complex, which keeps crashing back in to remind us of its status as frame. Both José and the prelude's Escamillo-associated fanfares seek to define closure on their own mutually exclusive terms. Carmen gets caught in the crunch.

The initial lines between Carmen and José are presented in secco recitative. Their first exchange (C: "C'est toi!"; DJ: "C'est moi!") establishes Carmen's openness, José's determination for finality. She explains in virtual monotone that her friends had warned her to avoid him, but that she decided "bravely" (the only flourish in her speech) not to flee. José enters haltingly to reassure and then plead. As he reveals his dream of running away with her, he returns to his characteristic urgency: rising sequences, straining intervals, the palpitating accompaniment of his "Flower Song." Eventually he reaches climax and rounds off his speech in C major with a sense of certainty. But Carmen responds dryly that she will not lie – their affair is over.

José meets her final pitch c^1 with his "Flower Song" syncopations, now in A♭. Again he argues that there is still time, that he

still loves her, that he can save them; and again his speech is a
perfect instance of lyrical bourgeois discourse, with sequential
build-up, climax and well-earned closure. Carmen answers, now
passionately: she knows he will kill her, but she will not submit.
José hears nothing: he repeats catatonically his previous A♭
speech, as though saying it will make it so. Carmen reiterates her
refusal at the same time. This is one of the few times they sing
together in the opera; significantly, they are completely at odds.

His syncopated accompaniment grinds to a halt as he finally
realizes that she does not love him. In response to his histrionic "Tu
ne m'aimes donc plus?," she answers simply "Non, je ne t'aime
plus," just as she shattered his declaration at the end of the "Flower
Song" ("Non, tu ne m'aimes pas"). Once again he seizes her final
pitch to pivot to a new key area, B♭ minor, where his urgency
becomes violent and agitated: he debases himself, promises anything, if only she will come with him. Carmen again resists and
declares valiantly her identification with freedom ("Libre elle est
née et libre elle mourra!"), pulling away from his B♭ minor to G
major. As she reaches her cadence, the opening material of the
prelude erupts (in G major) as the crowd inside the arena describes
the excitement of the bullfight. We are thus invited to understand
the events transpiring inside and outside the bullring as parallel,
although the particular mapping (who is bull, who torero in the
Carmen/José altercation) is left open. Finally, the crowd sings
"Victoire," urging Escamillo on to triumph.

The harmonic bass dissolves into a chromatic floor as the two
struggle. José, enraged by the accolades celebrating his rival, asks
Carmen point blank if she loves Escamillo. She halts the chromatic
slippage by confessing her love for Escamillo (V/D♭ major), at
which point the prelude materials enter on A major – Carmen's
cadential db^2 is respelled as $c\sharp^2$ and thus made consonant with the
crowd's enthusiastic recounting of Escamillo's triumph over the
bull. With the return of A major, we return to the key established
by the prelude and the previous scene. Escamillo's music seems
about to claim formal victory over the opera as a whole.

But the expected cadence on A is violently displaced by a
crashing C major triad. As José accuses her of laughing at him in
Escamillo's arms, his statements are punctuated by that aspect of
the prelude that involves him: his ensnarement with Carmen. She
orders him (D major) to kill her or let her pass. An E♭ fanfare
signals Escamillo's victory. José offers one more chance; she

responds by casting off his ring, rising to e♮^{2}. As José rushes at her ("Eh bien! damnée!"), he raises the ceiling to f^1, then f♯ ^{1}. But his triumphant cadence as he stabs her is greeted by the "Toreador Song" in F♯ major.[5] He succeeds in jacking the key up by half-step to this extreme realm, but has no influence on the materials that articulate his arrival except for a moaning countermelody. Even as he kills Carmen, Escamillo's swaggering theme mocks him.

The "Toreador" march leads into a series of F♯ major triads that hammer home the fatal prelude motive. José surrenders, confesses his crime, then indulges in one last moment of lyric urgency. As he finishes, a diminished seventh enters again to disrupt harmonic certainty. But it resolves to a splendidly ironic F♯ major, which sports a bright, affirmative mediant in the top voice. The opera concludes with two open octaves confirming F♯ with utter finality.

In this finale, Bizet gratifies simultaneously two very different notions of closure. On the one hand, José's dramatic and musical trajectories here reach climax and resolution: he has managed to possess Carmen, even if it has meant annihilating her. The instability of the final number encourages the listener both to fear his rage and to long for the event that will put an end to this turmoil. The urgency of Bizet's music, in other words, invites us to desire Carmen's death. But, on the other hand, the formal symmetries that had spelled normalcy throughout the opera and the promise of containment by the opening frame likewise achieve satisfaction here. The principal irony of the opera concerns a fatalism that engages with the most basic formal processes: the willful teleology of José's actions results in the "necessary" return of materials announced before he even appeared. His agency dissolves into the fulfillment of a fate foretold.

Yet for all the formal neatness of this conclusion, the specter of Carmen – the character who lent her vitality, her dissonance/dissidence to the proceedings – continues to resonate. We leave the theater humming her infectious tunes, and the closure that had seemed so indisputable opens up again. At what cost did we secure closure and certainty? It is because Bizet's closure is at once so absolute and yet so inconclusive that we return over and over again to this text. Chapters 6 and 7 will examine the wide range of readings *Carmen* has provoked.

6 *The reception of* Carmen

Reactions to the premiere

Ludovic Halévy realized on opening night that *Carmen* had failed (see his account in Chapter 2). A few days later, he assigned the blame to unfamiliarity: "It took a little time for [staff and performers] to get to like and admire this score. At the outset we were more astonished than enchanted by it. Such was the evident impression on the audience the first evening. The effect of the performance was uncertain, indecisive. Not bad, but not good either."[1]

If Halévy found it difficult to read the audience's cool response during the performance itself, he did not have to wait long to learn the grounds for its displeasure. While unfamiliarity no doubt played a role, it was by no means the principal problem cited by the reviews that began appearing immediately. Bizet's opera sparked antagonisms along two fronts: moral propriety and musical style. Given his boasts that he intended to "change the *genre* of *opéra-comique*" and the protests of the Opéra-Comique management over the project, the hostility with which *Carmen* was greeted in the press ought not to have been a surprise. Yet the response devastated Bizet, who is reported to have exclaimed during opening night: "Don't you see that all these bourgeois have not understood a wretched word of the work I have written for them?"[2]

The most ferocious of the attacks objected to the explicit portrayal of female sexuality in the opera, and the most abusive of these came from Jean-Pierre-Oscar Comettant and Achille de Lauzières, Marquis de Thémines. Comettant wrote:

Friends of unrestrained Spanish gaiety must have been delighted. There were Andalusians with sun-burned breasts, the kind of women, I like to think, who are found only in the low cabarets of Seville and lovely Granada. A plague on these females vomited from Hell! ... this Castilian

111

licentiousness! It is a delirium of castanets, of leers *à la Congreve*, of provocative hip-swinging, of knife-stabs gallantly distributed among both sexes; of cigarettes roasted by the ladies; of St. Vitus dances, smutty rather than sensuous ... To preserve the morale and the behavior of the impressionable dragoons and toreadors who surrounded this *demoiselle*, she should be gagged, a stop put to the unbridled twisting of her hips ...

The pathological condition of this unfortunate woman, consecrated unceasingly and pitilessly to the fires of the flesh ... is fortunately a rare case, more likely to inspire the solicitude of physicians than to interest the decent spectators who come to the Opéra-Comique accompanied by their wives and daughters ...

[Carmen enters as] *la terrible espagnole* who leaps like a tiger-cat, writhes like a snake ... ingenious orchestral details, risky dissonances, instrumental subtlety, cannot express musically the uterine frenzies of Mlle Carmen.[3]

Here we find signaled virtually all of the social tensions addressed in Chapter 3: the loathsomeness of the "Oriental" (here, the Andalusian), lower-class cabarets, prostitutes, the hip-swinging of exotic dance. Carmen becomes an animal (tiger-cat, snake) and is suspected of gynaecological disorders. Comettant focuses his disgust upon the character herself; Bizet and his collaborators are held responsible just for having brought such a creature before the public eye. The male characters – not only José, but also the soldiers and Escamillo – are described as "impressionable," ready victims for the *femme fatale*.

The misogyny that emerges in Comettant (his disgust with breasts, hips, uterine frenzies) is just as virulent in Lauzières, as is the contempt for the racial Other and the underclass:

This [the world of courtesans] is the class from which writers enjoy recruiting the heroines of our dramas, our comedies and even our *opéras-comiques*. And when once an author has become befouled in the social sewer, he is forced to descend ... to the lowest level for a choice of models ... He feels in duty bound to outbid his predecessors.

This "better" one ... is a "*fille*" in the most revolting sense of the word; a woman, mad over her body, giving herself to the first soldier who comes along, out of caprice, bravado, by chance, blindly. Then, after having lost him his honor, treated him with scorn, she deserts him to run after a handsomer fellow whom, in turn, she will leave when she likes. In the meantime she makes it her business to sleep with customs officials in order to facilitate the exploits of smugglers ... A savage; half gypsy, half Andalusian; sensual, mocking, shameless; believing neither in God nor in the Devil ... she is the veritable prostitute of the gutter and the crossroads.[4]

The line about "an author ... befouled in the social sewer" has been read as a personal attack on Bizet, an allusion to his liaison with Céleste Mogador. Later in the review, Lauzières exempts Mérimée from any responsibility, arguing that the novella represented a "phenomenon in the pathological library of a scholar," its excesses "the limbs or viscera ... revealed by an anatomist as he traces the ravages of gangrene" (p. 400). So long as the story was confined to the pages of élite literature, it did no harm. But when presented as public spectacle – especially at the Opéra-Comique – *Carmen* became intolerable: "At the Opéra-Comique, a subsidized theater, a decent theater if ever there was one, Mlle Carmen should temper her passions."[5]

Théodore de Banville wrote one of the few positive reviews of the opening. He recognized the same transgressions as the others, but chose to celebrate rather than to decry them:

The Opéra-Comique, the traditional theater of kind-hearted brigands, languorous maidens, rose-water loves, has been forced, violated, stormed by a band of unbridled romantics ... Either Seville ... the *posada* drenched in aloes, the oleanders and the cigarette-smoke ... Carmen murdered, bathed in her own blood, must disappear ... or *Fra Diavolo* must return to the vague regions of faded fabrications and empty shadows! All the more so because the bold attempt of the insurgents has left no door open for conciliation ... If we aren't careful they will end by so thoroughly corrupting our second lyric theater, formerly such a sweet, well-behaved child, that we shall even hear beautiful lines there, which would affect the late Scribe as a good bath in holy water affects the devil ...

Instead of those pretty sky-blue and pale-pink puppets who were the joy of our fathers, [Bizet] has tried to show real men and real women, dazzled, tortured by passion ... whose torment, jealousy ... mad infatuation are interpreted to us by the orchestra turned creator and poet ... To bring about such a *coup d'état* M. Bizet ... found the only associates who could have the idea, the courage and the audacity to give him enough range by throwing out the window all the old rubbish and old ghosts of the Opéra-Comique ... Take care, M. du Locle, M. Bizet, M. Meilhac, M. Halévy, for Lady Macbeth was right. In spite of all the perfumes of Araby the odor of blood will always be there. How in the future can ... *La Dame blanche* ... ever be brought back?[6]

This gleeful account of the demise of *opéra-comique* comforted Bizet in the midst of what was otherwise almost unrelieved condemnation. He wrote to Banville, "There is no way of thanking you for the charming article you devoted to *Carmen*. I am very proud to have inspired this delightful fantasy."[7] This fantasy matched, of course, his own earlier sense of his mission, before he became beleaguered by the consequences.

Content, however, was not the only component of *Carmen* critics found objectionable. The war over Bizet's Wagnerian influence erupted once again, and this time he found himself attacked from both sides. Writing from the anti-Wagnerian position, Léon Escudier wrote: "In *Carmen* the composer has made up his mind to show us how learned he is, with the result that he is often dull and obscure. He makes a point of never finishing his phrases till the ear grows weary of waiting for the cadence that never comes."[8] Baudouin characterized the opera as having "complete absence of light – music dwelling from start to finish in a limbo of greyness."[9] These qualities – learnedness, obscurity, greyness, endless melodies – were understood as Wagnerisms, the product of "one of the most ferociously intransigent of our young Wagnerian school."[10] But others saw Wagner's influence as positive. In praising *Carmen*, Banville expressly labeled Bizet as a Wagnerian "who is set against expressing passion in songs set to dance tunes," "for whom ... music must be, even in the theater, not an entertainment, a way of spending an evening, but a divine language expressing the anguish, the folly, the celestial aspirations of the being who ... is a wanderer and an exile here below."[11]

Yet some Wagner devotees faulted *Carmen* for being insufficiently Wagnerian. Ernest Reyer wrote:

While doing justice to the undeniable merit of the work, I regretted not finding in it a high enough affirmation of the doctrines the young composer professed ... He set himself to playing castanets and watching his rhythms. He wrote songs and *seguidillas* for Carmen, and for Escamillo "*Toréador en garde!*" In short he, the composer of *Djamileh* and *L'Arlésienne*, became the author of a Spanish *opéra-comique*. I cannot say that ... in *Carmen* one finds the culmination of Bizet's genius. Of his talent, at most.[12]

Likewise, Adolphe Jullien accused him of trying so hard to appease the followers of *opéra-comique* that he lost his integrity:

The composer has naïvely imagined that it would be enough for him to attenuate his preferences, repudiate his juvenile audacities, timid and modest as they were, rally openly to the traditional *opéra-comique genre*, whose sacred forms he had believed he could stretch or modify according to the exigencies of his libretti – in fact to write plenty of lively *couplets* and easily memorized refrains, in order to win those precious praises that most of the critics obstinately refused to bestow on him ... This *opéra-comique* is nothing but a long string of compromises.[13]

History would seem to have proved most of these positions wrong. It is easy to ridicule such reviews with the benefit of hindsight, to wonder at how so many critics could have missed the mark by such a margin regarding this, the most popular French opera in the repertory. But to castigate these readings by means of our own presumably more accurate ones shuts us off to the very important evidence provided by *Carmen*'s first interpreters. For they alone can indicate what Bizet's opera signified in his own context.

At the heart of each of the original reviews – whether pro or con, moralistic or stylistic – lies some crucial notion of difference. Comettant, Lauzières and Banville focus on differences of gender, race and class – the intrusion of female sexuality, an unwashed "Orient," the music of low-life dives – and the violated integrity of both *opéra-comique* as genre and the Opéra-Comique as institution. Banville applauded this assault on traditional values – as a bohemian writer who championed Realism, he welcomed the entry of this aesthetic into a terrain that seemed to him moribund. He located the significance of *Carmen* in its transgressions. None of these critics found it worthwhile to mention the theme of "fate" that later writers discovered.

Likewise those writers who concentrated on issues of style stressed difference rather than unity of style. The eclectic mix from which *Carmen* is composed was not only obvious to Bizet's contemporaries, but it occasioned bitter debate. Bizet's debt to German models was not at issue: the question was whether there was too much or too little Wagnerian influence. Likewise everyone pointed to the source of the "Spanish" passages as the cabaret, a site that was itself the subject of controversy. The Wagnerians objected to the banality of such music; traditionalists decried its lower-class origins. Nor was *Carmen* heard as a masterly fusion of diverse discourses. Most French commentators heard the score as a mishmash of unblendable elements.

Reception outside France

In the autumn of 1875, *Carmen* (newly outfitted with Guiraud's recitatives) opened in Vienna to great critical acclaim. It is from this moment that we can begin to chart the opera's popular success. Yet we should hesitate to judge that the Viennese were able truly to understand this work so misconstrued by the French, for their terms of reception were very different. The Viennese had no stake in the Opéra-Comique or its principal genre: no venerable Austrian institution was being attacked by *Carmen*. Thus the debate over generic propriety and venue did not recur on foreign soil. Likewise, many of the topical strands in *Carmen* – an Orientalism linked with colonialism, the prostitutes and bohemian dives that still smacked of the Commune in Paris – were not especially of concern outside France. And on the home turf of German music, nothing in *Carmen* recalled Wagner in the least. The opera was simply French; the whole score qualified as exotic. Thus, the *"Carmen"* embraced by the Viennese was not the same *"Carmen"* the Parisians had repulsed. In other words, the opera was finally only "understood" when its premises, its materials, its sources were no longer entirely intelligible.

Carmen attracted an impressive group of followers in Vienna, including many prominent composers and writers. Wagner himself is reported to have said of *Carmen*, "Here at last for a change is someone with ideas, thank God!"[14] He seems not to have noticed his own image in the music, however. Brahms likewise was an admirer. According to the testimony of Andrew de Ternant, Brahms told Debussy that he had attended twenty performances of the opera and "would have gone to the end of the earth to embrace the composer of *Carmen*."[15] He treated Debussy to a performance of the opera and explicated his favorite passages to him with great enthusiasm. Brahms is said to have ascribed *Carmen*'s greatness to its French qualities: "The French are the most cultured of the Latin countries, and this is reflected in their masterpieces of literature, art, and music. Bizet did not paint Carmen as a low-bred follower of Spanish soldiers, but as a bewitching, cultured woman of his own nationality."

Two particularly interesting accounts of the opera survive from figures outside France – by Tchaikovsky and Nietzsche – and these accounts reveal a good deal about the differences between French and non-French receptions. Tchaikovsky actually saw the original production at the Opéra-Comique on January 19, 1876. His brother Modest reported: "Rarely have I seen my brother so deeply moved by a performance in the theater . . . In [Galli-Marié's] performance, Carmen, while retaining all the vitality of her type, was at the same time shrouded in a certain indescribable magic web of burning, unbridled passion and mystic fatalism."[16] Tchaikovsky himself wrote, "I know nothing which in recent years has really seriously captivated me except *Carmen* and Delibes' ballet [*Sylvia*]. It's music without pretensions to profundity, but so delightful in its simplicity, so lively (not contrived but sincere) that I got to know it all almost by heart from beginning to end" (p. 59). Later he wrote at greater length:

In my opinion, [*Carmen*] is a *masterpiece* in the full meaning of the word – that is, one of those rare pieces which are destined to reflect most strongly the musical aspirations of an entire epoch ... It is as though [Bizet] says to us: "You don't want anything majestic, heavy and grandiose, you want something *pretty*, and here's a *pretty* opera for you." And, indeed, I know of no music that would have a stronger claim to be the embodiment of that element which I call *prettiness, le joli*. It's delightful and charming from beginning to end. There's an abundance of piquant harmonies, of completely new combinations of sound – but all this isn't simply an end in itself. *Bizet* is an artist who plays tribute to our present age, but he is fired with true inspiration. And what a wonderful subject for an opera! I cannot play the last scene without weeping; on the one hand, the people enjoying themselves, and the coarse gaiety of the crowd watching the bullfight, on the other, the dreadful tragedy and death of two of the leading characters whom an evil destiny, *fatum*, has brought together and driven, through a whole series of agonies, to their inescapable end. (p. 59)

The contrast between Tchaikovsky's reading of the opera and those of the French critics is striking. Where they heard pretension, he perceived simplicity, prettiness. It is not clear how Bizet would have accepted this latter characterization: in a sense, Tchaikovsky reduces *Carmen* back to adjectives associated with standard *opéra-comique*. Yet Tchaikovsky also acknowledges the dark side of the work. In Galli-Marié's performance he saw not scandal but vitality, passion, "mystic fatalism." The tensions of class, race and gender in the opera fall out of sight, and the mechanism responsible for the demise of the two lead characters is "evil destiny, *fatum*." "Fate" was, of course, an important concept for Tchaikovsky: the pessimistic program to his Fourth Symphony (1877) echoes his description of Carmen in its emphasis on evil destiny, the impotence of individual agency compared with "the coarse gaiety of the crowd."[17]

Nietzsche's account of *Carmen* appears at the head of *The Case of Wagner*. Far from perceiving Bizet as a fellow-traveler in the cult, Nietzsche hails him as Wagner's antithesis and uses *Carmen* to flagellate the master of the "endless melody":

Yesterday I heard – would you believe it? – Bizet's masterpiece, for the twentieth time ... How such a work makes one perfect! One becomes a "masterpiece" oneself ...

This music seems perfect to me. It approaches lightly, supplely, politely. It is pleasant, it does not *sweat* ... this music is evil, subtly fatalistic: at the same time it remains popular – its subtlety belongs to a race, not to an individual. It is rich. It is precise. It builds, organizes, finishes: thus it constitutes the opposite of the polyp in music, the "infinite melody." Have more painful tragic accents ever been heard on the stage? How are they achieved? Without grimaces. Without counterfeit. Without the *lie* of the great style ...

Has it been noticed that music liberates the spirit? gives wings to thought? ... Bizet makes me fertile. Whatever is good makes me fertile ...

This music is cheerful, but not in a French or German way. Its cheerfulness is African; fate hangs over it; its happiness is brief, sudden, without pardon. I envy Bizet for having had the courage for this sensibility which had hitherto had no language in the cultivated music of Europe – for this more southern, brown, burnt sensibility. – How the yellow afternoons of its happiness do us good! We look into the distance as we listen: did we ever find the sea smoother? – And how soothingly the Moorish dance speaks to us? How even our insatiability for once gets to know satiety in this lascivious melancholy!

Finally, love – love translated back into nature. Not the love of a "higher virgin!" No Senta-sentimentality! But love as *fatum*, as fatality, cynical, innocent, cruel – and precisely in this a piece of nature. That love which is war in its means, and at bottom the deadly hatred of the sexes! – I know no case where the tragic joke that constitutes the essence of love is expressed so strictly, translated with equal terror into a formula, as in Don José's last cry, which concludes the work:

"Yes, I have killed her / I – my adored Carmen!"[18]

For Nietzsche, Bizet's entire work – not merely the gypsy sections – constitutes the exotic Other, imbued as it is with "lascivious melancholy," African cheerfulness and fatal sexuality. Nietzsche hears no traces of the Wagnerism so deplored by the French, but he does notice – and luxuriates in – the Orientalist sensuality it provides, as well as the "tragic joke" of the "deadly hatred of the sexes." He goes on to argue that Don José's violent possessiveness has divine precedent: "Even God does not constitute an exception at this point. He is far from thinking, 'What is it to you if I love you?' – he becomes terrible when one does not love him in return." Having thus celebrated violent, egoistic possessiveness, Nietzsche adds sweetly: "You begin to see how much this music improves me? – *Il faut méditerraniser la musique*" (p. 159).

To be sure, we find out more here about Nietzsche's own proclivities than about *Carmen* itself. Yet certain elements of his account remain constant in subsequent moments of reception. Commentators continue to stress the formal simplicity of the music (earlier complaints of complexity disappear when the opera is juxtaposed with those of Wagner and others on the international stage), as well as its exotic and sensual pleasures. And many endorse his belief that the opera – its *femme fatale* and necessary murder – portrays finally the essential "truth" of sexual relations. It is a Darwinian truth, one "red in tooth and claw"; in that sense, at least, it represents *"fatum."* In Germany *Carmen* became metaphysical, the embodiment of perfection.

Responses in England were more varied. The 1878 premiere in London, for instance, produced some worldly, cynical reactions that contrast with both the moralistic reviews of the French and the hyperbole of the Germans:

Although Carmen is an even less respectable personage than the heroine of *La Traviata*, the plot of the opera is not openly offensive ... It is on Carmen herself that the weight of the opera falls. José, although he has plenty to sing, is a silly dupe, in whom little interest is felt: Escamillo is a conceited and brainless animal, and almost all the other personages are disreputable, except Micaela, of whom little is seen.

The heroine commands no respect and little sympathy, but the character has been so skilfully drawn, the wilfulness of the gay coquette is so piquantly painted, that the spectator is too much fascinated to inquire whether he is justified in giving her his smiles and his applause.[19]

George Bernard Shaw, on the other hand, was shocked when he saw *Carmen* performed in 1894 by his idol Emma Calvé. He begins, "the success of Bizet's opera is altogether due to the attraction, such as it is, of seeing a pretty and respectable middle-class young lady, expensively dressed, harmlessly pretending to be a wicked person, and ... anything like a successful attempt to play the part realistically by a powerful actress must not only at once betray the thinness and unreality of Prosper Mérimée's romance, but must leave anything but a pleasant taste on the palate of the audience."[20] He goes on to describe Calvé's Carmen as

a superstitious, pleasure-loving good-for-nothing, caught by the outside of anything glittering, with no power but the power of seduction, which she exercises without sense or decency. There is no suggestion of any fine quality about her, not a spark of honesty, courage, or even of that sort of honor supposed to prevail among thieves. All this is conveyed by Calvé with a positively frightful artistic power of divesting her beauty and grace of the nobility – I had almost written the sanctity – which seems inseparable from them in other parts. (p. 225)

Carmen in the canon

Within ten years of its premiere, *Carmen* had won a permanent place in the standard opera repertory. As its international success soared, even the French retracted their initial judgment, and the opera returned in triumph to the Opéra-Comique. Once again the management was nervous and tried to cast someone new in the title role; but Bizet's widow intervened on behalf of Galli-Marié, and it was she who presided over *Carmen*'s belated acceptance in Paris.

In striking contrast to its initial reception, *Carmen* came to be designated by many as a "perfect" opera.[21] Grout summarizes the qualities put forward in justification of *Carmen*'s exaltation thus: "Fundamental . . . is the firm, concise, and exact musical expression of every situation in terms of which only a French composer would be capable: the typical Gallic union of economy of material, perfect grasp of means, vivid orchestral color, and an electric vitality and rhythmic verve, together with an objective, cool, yet passionate sensualism."[22] Ernest Newman compares Bizet's achievement to the operas of Mozart: "It is the most Mozartian opera since Mozart, the one in which enchanting musical invention goes hand in hand, almost without a break, with dramatic veracity and psychological characterisation . . . This is indeed music muscled in the Mozartian way, the fascinating way of the cat-tribe, the maximum of power being combined with the maximum of speed and grace and minimum of visible effort."[23]

Canonization is not an unmixed blessing for an artwork, however. On the one hand, debates over worth subside, and extended circulation is guaranteed. But on the other, debates over meaning likewise recede in favor of quibbles over particular productions and performances. Whatever made the work initially seem strange, provocative or offensive grows dim, and unquestioned acceptance prevails. This happened even with *Carmen*.

To be sure, the illicit sexuality of the opera continues to be acknowledged; but as it took its place within the canon, *Carmen* became a locus for culturally-sanctioned titillation rather than a cause for moral indignation. A self-congratulatory smugness char-

acterizes much of what was written about *Carmen* after it became a
staple of the repertory, as subsequent critics gloat when recounting
the prudery of Bizet's initial audiences: "The libretto is effective,
but far from shocking a generation that now considers *Salome*
tame. The tragic ending is so seasoned a convention that we accept
it without thought."[24] The popular literature on *Carmen* (in album
notes, programs, surveys of favorite operas) tends to highlight the
elements of *femme fatale* and male victim, often rendering the plot
in a gleefully naughty, insinuating style.

But the widespread popularity of *Carmen* is not simply owing to
its lurid plot. Its wealth of vernacular-style tunes – initially so
controversial – ultimately contributed heavily to its success.
Carmen appeared just when the tensions between high and mass
culture were starting to emerge, and Bizet exploited those tensions
to great dramatic effect within the opera's framework. Yet Bizet's
intentions could not determine how his music would be understood, could not guarantee its integrity. And from the very outset,
the opera followed two radically different modes of reception. On
the one hand, this was seen as a composition that introduced
avant-garde Realism into the *opéra-comique*, and the intrusion of
popular styles into a "serious" genre counted as an extremely
transgressive act. *Carmen* is in some sense about this stylistic
violation and the formal need to purge the contaminating elements
from the fabric of the piece.

But on the other hand, because the opera is organized by means
of discrete numbers, those contaminating elements (easily the most
memorable and attractive moments in the score) could be lifted out
and recycled as ready-made kitsch. *Carmen* medleys – usually
composed of the "gypsy" numbers alone – began to appear almost
immediately. Sarasate's *Carmen Fantasy*, for instance, presents
arrangements of these tunes in the flashy gypsy-violin style so
fashionable at the time. Excerpted in this fashion, Bizet's melodies
became pop music, circulating through all levels of musical culture,
appealing to snobbish and entertainment interests alike.

Because of its double life, *Carmen* has proved effective in
recruiting new converts to "classical" music. Its story and catchy,
familiar music make it available to a mass audience, while its status
within the canon confers cultural prestige upon its fans: it serves as
a "hook" for attracting listeners to the pleasures of "high art." For
instance, Herbert Graf reports the following cluster of events
around 1948:[25] Flint, Michigan celebrated a local production of

Carmen by declaring Civic Opera Week "so that the people of Flint may show appreciation for the fact that our city has been recognized throughout the Nation as the outstanding leader and pioneer in the movement to establish completely civic opera in our own language in the cities of the United States" (p. 152); the New Orleans Women's Guild distributed excerpts of the opera to schools and ran essay contests, the prizes for which included Carmen dolls (p. 161); an all-children cast performed *Carmen* in Chicago. Yet at the same time *Carmen* was being used for civic hucksterism and music-education missionary work, a French film of *Carmen* was decried by the National Legion of Decency because of its "free love; suggestive situations; fatalism in theme; and irreverent references to religious matters" (p. 215).

Carmen's susceptibility to kitsch has sometimes worked against it in critical circles. As Herbert Lindenberger writes, "Verdi's name has been assimilated into a list [of 'great composers'] only in the last few years; certainly anyone who included Bellini, Bizet, or Puccini would risk intellectual embarrassment."[26] And indeed, the musicological literature often dismisses *Carmen* as a crowd-pleaser, unworthy of serious scrutiny. Those who undertake serious studies of *Carmen* tend to do so defensively, usually disregarding the sources of its popular appeal (its sexual improprieties, its use of cabaret music) and stressing "fate" or its avant-garde allegiance to Realism instead. For instance, Dahlhaus writes:

The work is a tragedy not simply because of its outcome, but because both Carmen and Don José, with a courage born of despair, shoulder a destiny which both secretly know will allow them no escape . . . There is between them the latent mutual understanding of the condemned, growing out of the dark awareness of an inescapable joint destiny in which each is the victim of the other . . . All the music in *Carmen* – the "on-stage" numbers, the expressions of despair to which there is no response, the stammered outbursts which meet with mockery – revolves around the dark centre where there are no words and where the tragedy of Carmen and Don José is really acted out.[27]

Such a reading is consonant with Dahlhaus' enterprise of depoliticizing the music of the canon. He salvages *Carmen* by ignoring issues of difference (class, race, gender, musical discourse) and emphasizing symmetry between the two principals, creating a quasi-formalist interpretation that does not refer outside its own boundaries.

Revisionist *Carmen*s

Most interpretations of *Carmen* either assume Carmen's treachery or else (as in Dahlhaus) try to eradicate the differences in class, race and gender between the two lead characters. But another group of readings accentuates those differences in order to lay bare the social power relations inscribed in the opera. Moreover, they often attempt to reverse those relations, inviting us to understand the work against the grain of its standard modes of reception.

There have been a few dissident voices in *Carmen*-reception all the way along. In the first cluster of reviews, Jullien rose to the defense of Carmen, arguing that her death was gratuitous, that José was responsible for his own downfall. Accordingly, he described the opera as "a vulgar *opéra-comique* with a dash of the pathetic and a final murder that is almost inexplicable."[28] As we have seen, Jullien's review was colored by his scorn over what he regarded as Bizet's disingenuous avant-garde posturing. Still, his interpretation set a precedent for later revisionist readings. Shaw too was appalled at the opera's finale – his description recalls "slasher" and "snuff" films:

Her death-scene, too, is horribly real. The young lady Carmen is never so effectively alive as when she falls, stage dead, beneath José's cruel knife. But to see Calvé's Carmen changing from a live creature, with properly coordinated movements, into a reeling, staggering, flopping, disorganized thing, and finally tumble down a mere heap of carrion, is to get much the same sensation as might be given by the reality of a brutal murder. It is perhaps just as well that a great artist should, once in a way, give our opera-goers a glimpse of the truth about the things they play with so lightheartedly.[29]

The twentieth century has seen a number of attempts at rereading *Carmen*. For instance, a 1925 revisionist production of *Carmen* in Moscow took the question of class in the opera and inverted its significance radically for purposes of the new revolutionary audience. As Frederick H. Martens describes it,

Carmen's cigarette factory stands in Polish Lodz where, while "rolling them" – she is a bright Jewish Communist girl instead of a gypsy – she uses her charms to win converts to Communism's cause. Her political instead of amatory activities get her in trouble with the authorities. Captain Joseph (once Don José), a police officer, is won over at the futuristic exhibition grounds where he was sent to arrest her, and lets her escape. He joins the smugglers bringing contraband ammunition into Russia; but when the girl loses her heart to a Polish wrestler instead of Spanish bullfighter, Joseph stabs him – and her, after she has uttered a fiery eulogy of Communism.[30]

Martens labels this and similar productions as "a perversion . . . the prostitution of famous operas as the carrying medium for Communistic doctrine in Soviet Russia, since the arbitrary separation of the music of an opera from its original story to make it a vehicle for the exploitation of political, economic, or any other form of propaganda is opposed to the fundamental ethics of musical art" (p. 440).

But *Carmen* was always about politics. What the Soviet *Carmen* accomplishes is a reversal of the usual terms. No longer is the audience positioned to identify with the bourgeois hero against the treachery of the underclass, ethnic (here, Jewish) female: in this production, our sympathies are guided towards the oppressed workers who heroically fight against injustice, proudly intoning something like the "Internationale" as they fall. Note that such a reversal of class sympathies is available in both Mérimée and Bizet without tampering, for Carmen often voices sentiments of class solidarity and functions effectively as a leader in the class struggle into which José blunders. It is in part her refusal of containment, her resistance to his claim of authority over her that gets her killed. As we saw in Chapter 3, the class tensions in *Carmen* were possibly perceived by the original audiences in terms of the Commune and the "necessary" reimposition of order by the bourgeoisie over the workers, and there is little doubt how most patrons of the Opéra-Comique would have identified. The Moscow production, however, played for an audience predisposed to identify the other way around.

Similarly, a 1984 production of *Carmen* at New York City Opera set the events within the Spanish Civil War, in which Carmen appears as a freedom fighter. This production too focuses the attention on political difference and predisposes the audience to sympathize with the plight of the character who resists military domination and fascist order. Because she stands on the disenfranchized side of the story's power relationships, Carmen's actions are revealed as the only strategies with which she can effectively defy oppression. When she dies, it is as a martyr to her people. Again, even without a change of setting, such a reading is available within Mérimée and the opera, for Carmen continually presents herself verbally in those terms. As Catherine Clément writes with respect to the opera,

Carmen the Gypsy. Therefore, somewhat whore, somewhat Jewess,
somewhat Arab, entirely illegal, always on the margins of life ... [E]very-
where [the Gypsies] went, they were subjected to the unerasable marks of
juridical and murderous exclusion ... So you can understand why she sings
for all she is worth about freedom. The freedom to travel ... is the freedom
to exist. A sedentary nomad no longer exists, and Carmen fights for the
right to live.[31]

However, productions of *Carmen* in Nazi Germany – which also
exploited the opera for the sake of the political tensions of the
moment – functioned to reinscribe (rather than to criticize) racial
hatred and the necessity of purging contaminating Others. And it
has been argued that some of the renewed interest in *Carmen* in the
last few years stems from growing resentment over the advances of
feminism and minorities. In these instances, the ambiguities of the
opera are resolved in the direction of the traditionally dominant
reading (Carmen as *femme fatale*, José as victim), but they infuse
that reading with an urgency bordering on moral imperative.

Most revisionist readings of *Carmen* today, however, are motivated by a desire to reverse traditional sympathies, and the
dimension of the opera most often subjected to revision is gender.
The last twenty-five years – with its tumultuous "sexual revolution," the emergence of Gay Liberation and the Women's
Movement, the development of feminist literary, film and art
criticism – have witnessed a thorough overhaul of assumptions
concerning sexual propriety and representation, many of which had
served to stabilize the gender politics of *Carmen*.

That *Carmen* has long stood as a moral lesson about the dangers
of female sexuality is evident from much of what has been written
about it from the very first Parisian reviews up to the present. As
anthropologist Michel Leiris puts it,

Carmencita – who stabs one of her companions in the cigar factory and
ridicules until he kills her, the wretch whom she has forced to desert;
mistress of a matador ... who dedicates to her the beast he is about to kill,
as to a bloodthirsty goddess for whom he must risk death – the lovely
Carmencita, before being murdered, is indeed a murderess.[32]

Paul Bekker's musings on the opera go so far as to identify Carmen
categorically as Woman:

This is love as a primitive force, possessed almost of the power of destiny in
classic drama ... [The lead characters] are here conceived absolutely
primitively – especially the woman ... The receptive nature of woman is

portrayed with uncanny realism in her change of tone as she addresses the passersby, José, Zuniga, the smugglers, Escamillo ... indeed the conception of woman as a primitive creature was never developed to such an extent out of the qualities of the voice itself.[33]

As these quotations and many others bear witness, the character Carmen has not been received as just a figment of Mérimée's and Bizet's imaginations, but as the very image of Woman. To many critics and fans throughout *Carmen*'s history, it has appeared obvious that promiscuous women deserve to die, and the opera's finale has seemed to confirm that notion of justice.

Indeed, the theme of Carmen as a sexually appealing corpse is often celebrated in visual images designed to advertize the opera. The poster for the first production (frontispiece) shows José holding the dead Carmen, her head thrown back and her breasts thrust aloft. And the cover of the Solti recording features a close-up of the blood-drained body of Carmen, which sports a lurid knife-wound – painted so as to resemble female genitals. Both of these recall the epigraph to Mérimée's novella, whereby woman has two good moments: in bed and in the grave. Even if many critics insist it is Carmen's energy that appeals to audiences, this tradition of displaying her fetishized cadaver betrays the fact that the promise of her death is a reliable commercial draw.[34]

Because *Carmen* has so often been read as a moral tale demanding the death of a woman who insists upon freedom – because it is always so heavily invested in sexual politics – feminists have identified it as a work most urgently in need of scrutiny. One of the more unexpected critiques of Carmen-as-corpse has been offered by the pop singer Madonna, who includes as one of her principal agendas the undoing of such images of female victimization. In some of her shows, Madonna dresses in Carmenesque costumes, falls as though dead and rises again triumphant.[35]

Clément's account of *Carmen* appears in a chapter called "Dead Women," which examines the narrative justifications for the deaths of several prominent opera heroines. She begins:

The most feminist, the most stubborn of these dead women is Carmen the Gypsy, Carmen the damned. Just the same, this woman who says no will die too. This woman who makes decisions all alone ... She is the very pure, very free, Carmen. My best friend, my favorite ... She is the image, foreseen and doomed, of a woman who refuses masculine yokes and who must pay for it with her life. (p. 48)

Clément identifies with Carmen – her energy, her strength, her independence, her sensuality. And she understands her heroine as doomed by her status as an ethnic outsider, as a woman and as a female character within a genre that demands death for purposes of closure:

You will see: opera heroines will often be foreigners. That is what catches them in a social system that is unable to tolerate their presence for fear of repudiating itself. This is how opera reveals its peculiar function: to seduce like possums, by means of aesthetic pleasure, and to show, by means of music's seduction (making one forget the essential), how women die – without anyone thinking, as long as the marvelous voice is singing, to wonder why. You will see: their foreignness is not always geographical; it appears in a detail, a profession, an age no longer said to be womanly. But always, by some means or other, they cross over a rigorous, invisible line, the line that makes them unbearable; so they will have to be punished. They struggle for a long time, for several hours of music, an infinitely long time, in the labyrinth of plots, stories, myths, leading them, although it is already late, to the supreme outcome where everyone knows they would have to end up.[36]

Here Clément appeals to the notion of "fate" that runs through the *Carmen* literature, but her interpretation of how *fatum* operates within the opera passes beyond the text of *Carmen per se* and into an indictment of the narrative conventions of nineteenth-century opera in general. By identifying publicly with the despised Carmen, she merges the personal and political in her critique. Towards the end of the book, she writes of her operatic heroines:

I identify with them, with them alone, their long battle, their fight; I will not bear their defeat much longer, the undoing that has begun again . . . I will be Carmen, and no one will understand the meaning of a "no." I will be multiple; I will disperse myself from music to music, secretly prey to unknown tenderness. I will turn myself over to femininity without reservation, but no one will know it. And their music inside me will be like night in the middle of the day. A perpetual eclipse of the male sun. (p. 176)

Nelly Furman, in her "The Languages of Love in *Carmen*," is likewise inclined to identify with Carmen, for many of the same reasons as Clément.[37] Early on in her essay, she presents a synopsis of the opera from Carmen's vantage point: "To thank him for letting her escape, Carmen, a gypsy, bestows her favors on José, a corporal in the dragoons. He falls in love with her, abandons the army, and joins the gypsies. When Carmen tires of him and his jealousy, she breaks off their relationship and becomes involved with a matador; José kills her" (p. 170). The usual account of the narrative is rearranged here, its causality subtly ruptured by the semicolon before the last three words.

Again, there is ample evidence within the novella and the opera in support of such feminist readings. Mérimée and Bizet grant power, courage and integrity to the character Carmen, while they portray José as lacking in moral fortitude. A contemporary audience (influenced by the Women's Movement, liberal sexual mores and sensitivity to issues involving spousal assaults) may be predisposed to side with Carmen against the irrational violence of José. Moreover, the original Carmen, Galli-Marié, collaborated closely and sympathetically with Bizet in order to realize this role to its fullest; she and many others have found it to be exceptionally fulfilling to perform. It has often been suggested that Bizet himself – who likewise felt constricted by the codes of his day – might have identified with his illustrious female character. While he never went so far as to utter (in the manner of Flaubert) "Carmen, c'est moi!," such a case can certainly be made.

But Furman resists the idea of accepting the terms of the opera and identifying with its lead character, whether she is perceived as monster or martyr. Instead, most of her essay is given to deconstructing (rather than merely reversing) the binarisms upon which the opera's text relies – rejecting the choices offered there and teasing out hidden tensions that effectively decenter the opera. As a literary scholar, she brings recent critical methods and issues to bear in a close reading of the libretto. She suggests that the plot might be seen not so much as the conflict *between* the sexes as *within* them, with Don José pitted against Escamillo, Carmen against Micaëla; she argues that "Carmen" might not truly be present at all except to serve as a foil for the antagonism between the two male leads or for the fueling of José's self-absorbed narcissism; she examines Carmen's linguistic virtuosity and compares it with José's very literal discourse which prevents him from understanding Carmen's delight in verbal play.

In short, Furman uncovers the unstable terms that construct the characters and plot in *Carmen*. Through this process, she opens the opera up to a variety of alternative readings, especially ones that break out of the master/slave duality that informs most traditional as well as many revisionist readings. Far from being a unified, organic entity, *Carmen* is here revealed as an assemblage of heterogeneous, often incompatible elements.

To admit that there are many mutually incompatible readings of the opera, however, is not to suggest that its meanings are thereby arbitrary or inconsequential. The passion with which critics have defended their positions throughout *Carmen*'s 115-year history indicates how well the opera serves as a social lightning rod. In a sense, the ongoing battle over its meanings itself constitutes its "meaning," which is always being modified, appropriated or disputed in keeping with the critic's or producer's interests and priorities. Thus if *Carmen* has no indisputable "truth" to impart, it has played and continues to play a vital role in the terrain of cultural representation: a terrain where images of gender, sexuality, class, race, ethnicity and art itself are fiercely contested. *Carmen*'s power lies not in its ability to inspire consensus, but rather in its success at provoking and sustaining debate along the central faultlines of nineteenth- and twentieth-century culture.

Neither Furman nor Clément deals directly with *Carmen* as a work that also includes music and dramatic action – their critiques focus almost exclusively on the words. Yet it is one thing to envision alternative readings of an opera by examining its libretto in isolation, and it is quite another to confront the work within the context of production: to see if, as a spectator, one can truly identify against the thrust of the text as it is usually construed or if, as a producer, one can cause this text to be perceived in new ways.

Four films based on *Carmen* appeared in 1983–4. Three of them relied heavily on Bizet's music, and each attempted to rechannel the power of Mérimée's and Bizet's constructs in new directions. Chapter 7 examines those films.

7   Carmen *on film*

It is difficult to overestimate the impact of *Carmen* on popular culture. The pseudo-Spanish costumes typical of *Carmen* productions regularly influence fashion design. Several contestants in the ice-skating competitions of the 1988 Olympics presented routines based on *Carmen*, and this inspired a full-length television production in 1990 called *Carmen on Ice*, featuring three Olympic champions in the leading roles. Cartoon versions of the opera indicate that *Carmen* is a standard touchstone of general culture, even for children. In an episode of *The Simpsons*, the family goes to the opera, where – what else? – *Carmen* is playing. Bart and Homer join in singing the contrafactum lyrics to the "Toreador Song" that must be nearly as old as the original: "Toreador / Don't spit on the floor / Use the cuspidor / That's what it's for."

But the principal site of *Carmen*'s entry into popular culture is film. Films of *Carmen* began to appear in 1910, with versions produced by both Pathé and Edison. In 1915 Cecil B. De Mille released a *Carmen* starring the opera-singer Geraldine Ferrar, a casting decision that enhanced the film with Ferrar's prestige alone, since the film was silent; and Fox responded with a version starring Theda Bara, the quintessential "vamp." Some of the more illustrious *Carmen* movies that followed include ones featuring Charlie Chaplin and Pola Negri (Lubitsch's *Gypsy Blood*) and Dolores del Rio (*The Loves of Carmen*). Technically speaking, all of these were silent films; but in practice, the familiar music was ever-present, performed by staff musicians at local cinemas. The first sound version of the opera appeared in 1931 (also titled *Gypsy Blood*), and by 1948, at least sixteen different *Carmen* films had been produced.[1]

As Jeremy Tambling argues in his discussion of *Carmen* films, each of these represents a rereading of the opera, inflected most obviously by prevailing attitudes concerning female sexuality at

130

each historical moment.[2] In several instances, women with genuine or purported ties to Mediterranean ethnic groups (Bara, Negri, del Rio, Rita Hayworth) were given *Carmen* as a vehicle to exploit the exoticism so central to their public personae. Each was billed as a *femme fatale*, with Bara's image as the most sinister of the group. But sinister faded into sultry and finally into pin-up glamor as the film industry became increasingly squeamish about erotica.

The era of sexual liberation has produced versions of *Carmen* far more explicit than anything ever imagined by Mérimée. A 1967 sex-exploitation film called *Carmen Baby* featured nudity and group-sex scenes. The 1980s contributed Juliet Bashour's *Kamikaze Hearts*, an extremely dark version of *Carmen* involving a lesbian couple who work in the pornographic film industry. Forced to witness the hard-core scenes enacted before the camera by her flamboyant lover, Tigger ("José") becomes violently jealous. While the script stops short of the anticipated murder, the pervading sense of despair at the end of the film is nearly unbearable. Bizet's music makes cameo appearances throughout the film – at one point, the characters are shown filming a pornographic version of *Carmen* with the star singing the "Habañera" – most of the film is a rereading of Mérimée's themes translated into a lesbian subculture.[3]

In fact, most of the films mentioned so far draw more on the sensationalist elements of Mérimée's story than the opera itself, although the ever-popular music appears regularly for the sake of color and as a means of referring to the realm of "high art." But a few *Carmen* films engage more directly with Bizet's music. I have chosen four to discuss in some detail: Otto Preminger's film of Hammerstein's *Carmen Jones* (1954), Carlos Saura's *Carmen*, Peter Brook's *La Tragédie de Carmen* and Francesco Rosi's *Carmen* (all three from 1983–4).[4] None of these counts as a straightforward filming of the opera itself, but rather as a merger among the conventions of opera, cinema, theater, dance and much else. Yet each of them – through its *mises-en-scène*, alterations, inclusions and exclusions – sheds light on the opera, and each bears witness to the power of performative interpretation to reconstrue standard texts.

Hammerstein and Preminger: *Carmen Jones*

Carmen Jones began its life as a Broadway musical (1943–4), with lyrics and adaptation by Oscar Hammerstein II. Part of Hammerstein's motivation was populist in nature: to make opera accessible to American audiences.[5] But his decision to relocate Bizet's opera within a black American context also reflects his considerable business acumen. Hammerstein had discovered from the success of his earlier musical *Showboat* and Gershwin's *Porgy and Bess* that audiences responded enthusiastically to representations of blacks in music-theater, especially when the music appeared (to white ears, at any rate) to incorporate elements drawn from African-American genres. Such shows displayed a liberal agenda: to "elevate" the themes of the black community into "high art," to demonstrate the bonds of common humanity between races.

Carmen seemed the perfect vehicle for Americanization: the music and story were already familiar and popular to a large audience, and the opera itself raises racial issues. Hammerstein took the factor of race in the original as a starting point and made the entire cast black, offering the following rationale:

I want to establish that my choice of Negroes as the principal figures in the story was not motivated by any desire to pull an eccentric theatrical stunt. It is the logical result of my decision to write a modern American version of *Carmen*. The nearest thing in our modern American life to an equivalent of the gypsies in Spain is the Negro. Like the gypsy, he expresses his feelings simply, honestly, and graphically. Also as with the gypsy there is rhythm in his body, and music in his heart.[6]

This choice has complex ramifications. By eliminating racial difference from the work, Hammerstein also eliminates that as one of the reasons for Carmen's death. Seen from this angle, the piece becomes perhaps less racially-oriented than the original; gender and sexual propriety remain as the sole tensions organizing the plot. But the decision may reflect *increased* race-consciousness: American audiences of the 1940s and 1950s would not have tolerated a relationship between a white man and a black woman on stage or screen. The miscegenation central to the original story could not be transported into the American context.

In any case, if race is eliminated as a factor on one level, it returns all the more forcefully on another: Hammerstein resolves the split between Self and Other in such a way that the whole cast now stands as exotic for the gaze of a mostly white, affluent audience. In the quotation above, Hammerstein reiterates the old images of the black as simple, with "rhythm in his body." Likewise, Carmen's promiscuity, Joe's (José's) violence, Cindy Lou's (Micaëla's) rural ignorance, Husky Miller's (Escamillo's) prowess as an athlete and

Frankie's (Frasquita's) bawdy cabaret style of singing all fall comfortably in line with and reinscribe stereotypes of African-Americans. The show maintains an uneasy tension: are these characters to be read as "universal" (that is, is a white spectator to perceive them as "just like us")? Or do they reveal black idiosyncrasies? Throughout his book, Hammerstein shifts nervously between these positions.

The story has been rearranged with apparent ease. Joe is a serviceman aspiring to become a pilot; Cindy Lou is his girlfriend from home; Carmen works in a parachute factory; Husky Miller is a boxing champion. Mérimée's plot runs quite smoothly in this context, and only a few details are changed to accommodate it. For instance, given that José should murder Carmen in a way that parallels Escamillo's defeat of his opponent, Joe kills Carmen with his hands – strangling rather than stabbing her. And Hammerstein's Carmen is not an outlaw; she runs off to Chicago to help Joe escape punishment for having knocked out his senior officer and to be with her friends, members of Husky's entourage.

The adaptation of Bizet's music to this new context, however, is somewhat uncomfortable. In many instances (especially in passages not marked as exotic in the original), the characters sing music that is more or less straight opera. It is identified as African-American only by virtue of the occasional "dat" or colloquialism (in his "Flower Song," Joe sings "Dere all de same, she jus' a dame"). Moreover, Preminger's film actually has several of the parts sung by white opera-singers, thereby preserving European qualities of operatic vocal production.

But the results of this dubbing are often strange. Carmen's part (played by Dorothy Dandridge) is sung by Marilyn Horne, with a thin, reedy sound instead of the voice Horne usually uses for Carmen. It is as if Horne, who was brought in to sing a part presumably beyond the capabilities of the black actress, were trying to produce a sound quality she identified with untrained singers, so as to give the illusion of authenticity. Horne's runs in the "Seguidilla" ("Dere's a café on de cor- - - - -ner") sound suspiciously sloppy, again as though the producers assumed that since "Carmen Jones" could not be expected to negotiate such ornaments, Horne would need to smear them. Likewise, Harry Belafonte's Joe hovers uneasily between a halting, breathy style that maintains the "realist" illusion that this is a black soldier singing and the heroic sweep required by the latter sections of the "Flower Song."

The tensions are even more telling in the "exotic" sections of the score that must have attracted Hammerstein to *Carmen* in the first place. The "Habañera" and "Seguidilla" present few problems, since the signs of "Oriental" exoticism have long been used in film to represent alluring feminine sexuality. But the appeals and dangers of this kind of cross-cultural adaptation show up strikingly during the scene at Billy Pastor's (Lillas Pastia). Carmen arrives at Pastor's place to the strains that open Act II of the opera, and as the camera enters the room, we see couples jitterbugging to Bizet's pseudo-flamenco music. Hammerstein invites a comparison between the gypsy cabaret (already a heavily mediated cultural site in Bizet's work) and a black juke-joint. In both cases, rhythmic music inspires uninhibited dancing. But the grooves do not match: no one could jitterbug to Bizet's music, which incongruously displaces the swing music associated with the physical gestures executed by these dancers.

At this moment, Bizet's music suddenly gives way to a drum solo – the kind of savage eruption Gene Krupa (a white drummer) used to favor in order to display his empathy with black "primitivism," even though black drummers rarely play in this fashion. The jungle drums introduce Pearl Bailey – the only member of the cast who brings a colloquial style of singing with her into this alien realm – who sings "Beat out dat rhythm on a drum," a reworking of Carmen's gypsy song. On the one hand, it is a relief to hear something resembling African-American performance style, as Bailey shapes the tune with her own splendid inflections. But on the other hand, we have to hear her participating in pseudo-dialect and testifying to the innate relationship between drums and black bodies. It is in this scene that Hammerstein strives to prove the rightness of his translation from Bizet's gypsy Spain to the black communities of the South, and it is this scene that now may seem most contrived, most overtly racist, for it reveals all too clearly the assumptions that inspired this fusion in the first place.

Nonetheless, there is much to recommend *Carmen Jones*. The marvelous cast (Dandridge, Belafonte, Bailey, Diahann Carroll) presents the drama with more conviction than is typical in opera productions. This radical recontextualization also produces something of an "alienation effect": the fit between story and music that can seem "natural" here seems strange, available for new insights. In particular, the experiment of changing the racial dimension of the piece – while finally exceedingly problematic – may encourage us to reconsider *Carmen* in terms of racial politics and cultural representation.

Carlos Saura: a flamenco *Carmen*

The film directed by Carlos Saura likewise highlights the issue of ethnicity. The Spanish have always denied that Bizet's *Carmen* has anything to do with Spain, and in Saura's production, Bizet's representations of flamenco are self-consciously juxtaposed with the music and dance of genuine flamenco artists. Other films influenced this project: a couple of years earlier, Saura and the choreographer/dancer Antonio Gades had produced a highly successful flamenco version of a play by García Lorca, *Blood Wedding*. And Gades was responsible for choreographing the dance scenes in Rosi's film of the opera, in production concurrently with his collaboration with Saura.

The film unfolds on two narrative levels. Antonio (Gades) directs a flamenco company. He is preparing a production of *Carmen* based primarily on Mérimée, although he also listens to a tape of Bizet's opera. At the beginning, he is presiding over a dance class, searching for someone who could satisfactorily play the title role. A colleague leads him to another school, where he finds his ideal Carmen – an undisciplined, self-possessed young woman (fortuitously named Carmen) who has the "eye of the wolf" Mérimée ascribes to his heroine. Antonio invites her to join his troupe and teaches her to enact his vision of Carmen as *femme fatale*.

He soon falls desperately in love with her, Pygmalion-style, and the two narrative strands (their relationship, Mérimée's story) become confused – both to Antonio and to the spectator, who is often given mixed cues as to whether the action concerns *Carmen* or the affair between Antonio and his protégée. Like José, Antonio discovers that Carmen sleeps with other men, that she has a husband in prison, that she refuses to be controlled. His jealousy invades rehearsals, demoralizing the troupe, until it explodes in a scene in which she may be flirting either *within the production* with the torero or at a cast party with the man who plays the torero. When Antonio/José can stand it no longer, he pursues Carmen offstage; as the soundtrack plays the relentless final scene of the opera, he stabs her. But it remains unclear which narrative level contains the murder: as Antonio returns to the rehearsal space, the other members of the troupe are sitting around relaxing, as though what we witnessed was just a trial run of the production's final scene, rather than the murder of Antonio's lover who has been playing the part of Carmen. We are left not knowing.[7]

Bizet's music appears intermittently throughout the film, though neither in its original order nor as canonized text. It is subjected to reworkings and reinterpretations all the way along. For instance, the first operatic excerpt we hear accompanies the credits; but instead of the expected prelude, we are given the Act I chorus in which the women describe the fight between Carmen and Manuelita. Later in the film, we witness a flamenco staging of that fight; consequently, this excerpt – if it appears at all – must be placed elsewhere. But used as an introduction, this excerpt sets a violent, conflicted affect, in contrast to the "Spanish holiday" of Bizet's prelude. We are not invited to suppose that what we are about to watch will be bright and sunny.

The flamenco troupe includes a number of superb traditional musicians, who ordinarily provide the music for production numbers. Near the beginning of the film, as the musicians are rehearsing their own music, Antonio begins playing his tape of the "Seguidilla." The two proceed simultaneously for a while, until the musicians stop. A guitarist starts to improvise on the Bizet, converting this piece of pseudo-flamenco music into the genuine article. This requires changing the rhythmic impulse, and the musicians seem pleased with the results. But Antonio (who repeatedly betrays his disloyalty to his native style in his obsession with Bizet) insists that they compromise, even though they advise him that no one could dance to Bizet's tune.

Many critics have observed that Bizet never has José and Carmen sing together. Saura's film overcomes this "problem" by using the Act III entr'acte music to represent the tenderness experienced briefly by Antonio and his Carmen. In the context of the opera, this lovely moment featuring flute and harp stands as filler; but in Saura's film, it is this tune (rather than the "Seguidilla," which has already been used to deconstruct "exoticism") that plays while Carmen seduces Antonio. It invades both levels of the film's narrative, contributing to the confusion: it appears when Antonio and Carmen consummate their affair, and twice more when she tries to persuade him of her fidelity in the face of his jealousy. This entr'acte melody becomes the motive that Bizet denies Don José – the only principal in the opera who lacks a signature theme.

But the most stunning scenes of Saura's film are the ones in which the story is relayed exclusively through flamenco music and dance. These include a scene in the cigar factory, in which a group of women (some of them old, with beautiful, weathered faces) beat rhythmically on tables while singing a traditional strophic song. The tension escalates to the outbreak of the knife fight, where it stops in silence. Another is the scene in which the lovers have their first assignation, in which it is Antonio who dances for Carmen, rather than the reverse. If the body and dance were attributes of Carmen alone in the opera, this film assigns these qualities to both leads, creating a symmetry of grace and power between them. And the scene in which Antonio/José and the torero fight their duel is a masterpiece of aggressive machismo.

Saura's film presents a brilliant commentary on "exoticism": on the distance between actual ethnic music and the mock-ups Bizet and others produced for their own ideological purposes, on the domestication of traditional styles (especially of rhythmic impulse and aggression) for purposes of "art." Moreover, Saura reverses one of the central themes of the opera: if in Bizet's *Carmen* the seductive quality of the gypsy popular music causes José to abandon his discourse of "high art," in the film, the prestige of Bizet's music and the power of Mérimée's story lure Antonio away from his community (its music, its wisdom) and into an obsession that destroys both him and his lover.

Peter Brook: *Carmen* as structure

Peter Brook's reworking of *Carmen* premiered in Paris at the Théâtre Bouffe du Nord in 1981. Brook intended his *La Tragédie de Carmen* to strip away the layers that had stultified what he takes to have been Bizet's original vision. He began with the libretto itself:

Mérimée was an extremely economical writer, a minimalist who wasted no words and got right to the point. Bizet's music is also exquisitely to the point, in human terms. But the librettists brought to the opera's story a superstructure that was anti-Mérimée, totally decorative. Mérimée wouldn't use one showy phrase for its own sake, but his story, turned into an opera, has all these extras, these choruses, to make it palatable to audiences of the time. And it became a "Spanish show."[8]

Brook and his collaborators (composer-conductor Marius Constant and playwright Jean-Claude Carrière) reduced *Carmen* to what they perceived as its basic elements and reconstituted the opera, so that the story seems at once familiar and alien: "We are doing a new investigation of [*Carmen*] – hence the new title – and what we have done is to separate its central core from the rest of the material, like boning a fish. Everything is trimmed away to focus on the intense interaction, the tragedy of four people" (p. 13).[9]

The structural paradigm of the love triangle motivates *La Tragédie*. Bizet's opera contains two principal rivalries (José–Carmen–Escamillo; Carmen–José–Micaëla), while Mérimée's novella includes several other triangulations (Carmen and José as stable factors, with the third position filled variously by her husband Garcia, an English Milord, the Frenchman narrator and so on). Brook seizes this structure and presents the story as a series of permutations that rotate mechanically, each time leaving one "odd man out."

Thus the opening establishes the duality of José and Micaëla, into which Carmen intrudes, leaving Micaëla alone. Act II takes place in Lillas Pastia's one-woman brothel, as Pastia and Carmen ply with drink and seduce Zuniga, Don José and Escamillo in turn. The process is virtually identical each time, and Carmen even retreats upstairs with her pimp Pastia, only to return to José at the end of the scene. The third act introduces her husband Garcia, who is killed in short order, and Micaëla, whom José leaves alone with Carmen. And the fourth act revolves around Escamillo and the reentry of José. When Escamillo dies in the bullring, Don José and Carmen depart as if in a trance. Carmen submits to what seems like ritual sacrifice, and José is left alone: after Escamillo's demise, nothing remains to further the plot, and the other points of the triangle simply disintegrate.

In this structuralist rendition of the opera, Brook puts fate at the center in a way that recalls Nietzsche: "love as *fatum*, as fatality, cynical, innocent, cruel – and precisely in this a piece of nature. That love which is war in its means, and at bottom the deadly hatred of the sexes!" (see Chapter 6). The mathematical configurations sustaining *La Tragédie* resemble a game of billiards. There is no motivation, no agency here. The social presence so prominent in Bizet's opera is gone, leaving only this chain of triangles as a universal condition. The actors walk somnambulantly through their paces, cogs in a bloody Darwinian machine.

Unlike some reworkings of operas in which the music is sacrificed to theatrical realism, Brook has his characters sing Bizet's music.

But the music has been altered in a variety of ways. First, the orchestra contains only fifteen members.[10] The flair of the original score is subdued to ensure that it does not pull us into the dramatic sweep of the opera, away from our attention to structure. At certain crucial moments (e.g., Carmen's fatalistic "En vain" air from Act III or the beginning of the final duet), a piano replaces the orchestra altogether. Similarly, ominous solo timpani provide the stark support for the "Habañera." These choices all have the effect of alienating those passages of the opera for which our reflexes are most automatic.

Brook's version eliminates the sections extraneous to his vision of the opera, including all the choruses, and most of the remaining sequences are radically reordered. For instance, Bizet's prelude appears only once – at the beginning of Act IV, as Escamillo prepares for his final bullfight (the "fate" motive is thus attached principally to *his* destiny). Brook substitutes as opening music Carmen's "En vain," played on unaccompanied cello. The work is thus somber from the outset: the irony of Bizet's festive music in conjunction with the eventual tragedy is lost, but the rigor of Brook's concept is effectively foreshadowed.

While this melancholy music plays at the beginning of the film, a blanketed figure sits in the center of a dusty courtyard, watching and casting spells. Micaëla enters and sings her lines in which she asks after Don José. The sinister figure cackles and grabs her hand to tell her fortune. When José returns, Micaëla launches into their duet; but as he sings his reminiscence of his mother, the figure throws off the blanket to reveal an amused and unusually male-volent Carmen. She interrupts the duet with her "Habañera," captivating José by playing suggestively with a cigar. Her number is all the more sinister because of its bare timpani support. When Micaëla returns to try to win José back, the two women lunge at each other in a vicious, hair-pulling fight, accompanied by the music with which the altercation in the factory is depicted in the opera. Manuelita has been replaced here by Carmen's only true rival, Micaëla, and it is she whom Carmen scars with her knife.

Act II, with its play of triangles in the brothel, rearranges Bizet's sequence most severely. The seduction of Zuniga takes place against Carmen's "Gypsy Song" music. As José enters, the orchestra plays his plaintive passage from Act IV, "Je ne menace pas, j'implore, je supplie." Otherwise most of the music for Bizet's Act II encounter between Carmen and José occurs in this production as well, except that José is interrupted before his "Flower Song" by the angry return of Zuniga, whom he murders. Only then does Escamillo enter and sing his "Toreador Song." José challenges him to fight, and the duel/duet between the two men from Act III occurs. As Escamillo leaves, Pastia pulls Carmen upstairs to bed with him, leaving José alone to sing the "Flower Song" to himself. Carmen returns, hears its conclusion and joins with him in a passionate kiss that closes the act. Whereas in the opera, José's love song falls apparently on deaf ears, Brook's version yields to sentiment: the "Flower Song" achieves its desired end here, and we witness José and Carmen temporarily in accord.

A couple of other moments of rearrangement will have to suffice for this discussion. As Micaëla sings her Act III air, Carmen joins in with a countermelody based loosely on her own air concerning fate; and when José then leaves the two women together, we see them unified in their apprehension rather than as antagonists. The ending must also be changed, owing to Escamillo's death. The duet between Carmen and José thus concludes with her "Libre elle est née et libre elle mourra!" They watch Escamillo's body being carried away, to newly composed music based on the "fate" material from the prelude, and then leave the arena, again to the solo cello playing her fatalistic Act III air, "En vain." As they kneel for the execution, the ominous timpani reappear, obsessively playing the "Habañera" rhythm. This is all that remains of their history together.

While Brook clearly takes substantial liberties with Bizet's opera, virtually all of his shifts cast an interesting light back on the original. After seeing his production, those same moments in the context of the opera resonate differently. And for an opera as familiar as *Carmen*, this is quite an accomplishment. He returns to *Carmen* the dread, the unsettling feelings experienced by some of the opera's first audiences.

When Brook's production was broadcast on television, the enthusiastic commentator proclaimed Carmen "a liberated woman, in charge of her own life and own fate." But Brook's vision would seem to suggest quite the opposite: his Carmen is overtly a witch, a prostitute, an evil presence. She has no community (no choruses) to sustain her, and her submission to fate and death scarcely marks her as liberated. The interpretation is formalistic, ahistorical, apparently apolitical, as are most reflections on "fate" and "the human condition." David Wills writes, "In spite of the success of the production in making opera into convincing theater and not just an outmoded form of melodrama, I would read Brook's *Carmen* as something of a retreat from the issue of sexual politics which the text inevitably raises."[11] But in the 1990s, Brook's portrait of Carmen and her demise counts not simply as a retreat, but as a reaction against the advances won by women in the last two decades. The rigid law of Brook's triangulations – the tarot cards he metes out to Carmen – will admit of no agency, no license.

Francesco Rosi's *Carmen*

Several critics expressed surprise when Francesco Rosi, widely known for overtly political cinema, appeared as director for an opera – especially one as hackneyed as *Carmen*.[12] But Rosi's version of *Carmen* is simultaneously the most faithful to and most subversive of the opera as it is usually understood. Faithful because the production presents the musical score more or less without deviation – he does not rewrite or update the action, as do most revisionist adaptations. And subversive because his *mise-en-scène* succeeds in revealing and inverting the forceful political dimensions of this opera, the power relations surrounding class, gender, and race or ethnicity. Rosi's decision to stick with the score and libretto limits the extent to which he can overturn the opera. In order to circumvent the dictates of those highly determined elements, he exploits moments that have no specified content: instrumental interludes (against which he constructs montages that frame sub-sequent action) or inserted periods of silence.

Perhaps his most brilliant stroke occurs at the very outset, prior to the playing of the prelude. The film begins in a crowded arena where a bullfight is nearing completion. The scene presents a society that derives collective pleasure from watching the ritual of a hero conquering a dangerous force of nature. But the film-viewer is situated rather differently from the people in the stands, for the camera focuses almost exclusively on the bull. The bull is shot in close-up slow motion, so that his every move seems labored. Several gaudy lances already protrude from his back, and blood bathes his sides. His face is weary, uncomprehending. He does not want to be here. On the soundtrack, festive music blares in the distance, and spectators roar their approval of the torero's skill, as he goads the unwilling bull into half-hearted charges. Finally "the moment of truth" arrives – the moment that seals the event: for the first time, we see the torero's face (from the bull's perspective), as he aims his sword for the kill. As the sword penetrates the bull, the celebratory music of Bizet's prelude begins.

Rosi here raises the issue of spectacle and ritual murder most powerfully. He refuses to grant us a couple of hours of innocent fun before the story of *Carmen* (which we all know in advance) becomes lethal: he forces us to recognize that we too have come to witness and celebrate a ritual slaying. By positioning us so that we identify with the bull – the torero's preordained victim – however, he renders the opera's plot uneasy before it even starts, for we are aware that *Carmen*'s bloody conclusion occurs in conjunction with a bullfight. Rosi does not, for all that, dictate how we are to read the terms of the plot. Some perceive the bull as José, who is goaded mercilessly until he charges – in this reading, killing the torero Carmen. But, as we saw in Chapter 6, it is Carmen's death we have assembled to watch, and she (like the bull) has been depicted as a dangerous force of nature who must be contained. As a third possibility, Tambling suggests that the bullring represents an exclusively male world in which all women (by definition disenfran-chized) must angle and negotiate for survival.[13] Regardless of how one reads this opening, Rosi indicates that the stakes are high. No more than any of his other films is this entertainment or self-contained art.

The film's credits roll during the first two sections of the prelude, and behind the credits we see the aftermath of the bullfight: the mutilation of the bull, the adulation of the torero (later identified as Escamillo) by male fans, the women watching admiringly from the stands. Suddenly, the music breaks off. The scene changes abruptly from the glare and noise of the bullring to a night-time religious procession. Men in penitential garb march silently by, as spectators watch from their windows. The inflections of traditional lament float in the air, along with the chime of bells carried by the participants. This Spanish soundscape is shattered by the prelude's final section, with its melodramatic *frissons* and Orientalist aug-mented seconds. Onscreen, we see the appearance of a float bearing a statue of the Mater Dolorosa. Women (including the actress who plays Carmen) crowd around the statue, cheering with joy. As Bizet's music ends with its unresolved dissonance, the scene vanishes.

This part of Rosi's opening strategy serves several purposes. First, it immerses us in an ethnic culture alien to most viewers: this –

not the flashy mock-ups produced by generations of set-designers – is Spain. Here and throughout the film, Rosi denies us our beloved French version of Andalusia. His naturalist setting of this "Realist" opera ruptures preconceptions. Second, he causes this music to be associated with the dark side of Spain, rather than with "fate" or Carmen. Carmen is thus freed of this motivic baggage, and it becomes possible to see her as an individual, rather than as what the prelude has already labeled as the *femme fatale*.

This realignment of significations is more complicated than Rosi's bullfight sequence. For Carmen's first entrance in the opera is marked with that motive, and her first encounter with José brings back this section of the prelude. By assigning different associations with this music when we first hear it in the prelude, Rosi diminishes the likelihood that we will track that motivic web as it unfolds "fatefully" throughout the opera. But Rosi is explicitly concerned with replacing the centrality of "fate" in this opera with issues of power and responsibility:

Carmen is a woman who defends her dignity, her femininity. I was always skeptical, when I saw *Carmen* on the stage, about the idea of fate. According to me, on the contrary, Carmen fights *not* to die, but when she understands that in order not to die, she will have to lie, to deny her love for another man, then she accepts death; otherwise, she would lose her dignity. But it is not true that she submits herself to destiny.[14]

Thus it is no accident that Rosi refuses to grant the "fate" motive its usual privileged role as an omniscient herald of doom.

The principal means by which Rosi subverts the terms of the opera involve his realistic settings. From the very beginning of Act I, where we see a procession of shabbily dressed female laborers on their way to the cigar factory, Rosi insists that we see the extraordinary imbalances in economic, sexual and ethnic status within this world. The abject poverty of the native population (whom we observe in squalid camps on the outskirts of town) contrasts strongly with the imposing alabaster fortress and gold-trimmed uniforms of the occupying army. The soldiers look down upon this population with amused contempt; they are of a very different social order from the peasants passing in the streets.

Similarly, during the playing of the entr'acte before Act II, Rosi shows us several dramatically contrasting scenes: soldiers on guard duty; a party at an aristocratic palace where flamenco dancers perform for the pleasure of the guests (among whom is Escamillo);

the noisy interior of Lillas Pastia's proletarian tavern, which contains patrons ranging from gypsy families to soldiers who have come to drink and solicit native women. The film never lets us forget the centrality of class, imperialism and sexism to the organization of this society. These characters cannot be understood as autonomous individuals: their subject positions are constituted in terms of these various power relations.

The first few scenes also establish superbly the differences in culture between the army and the indigenous population. If Bizet's exotic music was drawn from Parisian cabarets and was used for aligning Carmen with the "Orient" and physical sensuality, Rosi recasts this music as traditional ethnic music. This is not to say that the music mysteriously becomes authentic. But Rosi films these portions of the opera as though they were the customary expressions of the gypsies when they are at leisure. The "Cigarette Chorus," for instance, is sung by the female factory workers on their break. They return to their enclave and perform within that context for themselves and their own families. That their sensuality is thoroughly accepted within the community is made clear when an elderly couple joins them in a hauntingly erotic dance (choreographed by Gades). Although a few soldiers look on, the women do not dance for their benefit: they are intruders, tolerated only because of the power they wield.

Consequently, when Carmen enters it is not as a *femme fatale*, but as a member of this community. The "Habañera" becomes a well-performed song, which soon has the entire group dancing and singing. Unfortunately, Don José witnesses her dance and systematically misreads all its signs. As Rosi presents it, her decision to throw the flower at him stems from his having prudishly dismissed the other soldiers. When she lures him forward and then casts the flower, she is perceived by her compatriots as having defied oppressive authority, and they respond with derisive laughter. In this production, the ease with which Carmen fits into her traditional community and its standards of pleasure prevents her from being seen as a *femme fatale*, even if she is more flirtatious and high-spirited than the other women. The problem arises with José's inability to deal with a woman whose cultural habits include sexual license.

But Rosi faces a dilemma here. In order to recontextualize Carmen as an actual gypsy, he has to present as ethnographically valid both Bizet's pseudo-gypsy music and the notion that lower-class and gypsy women are less inhibited sexually than their bourgeois sisters in the north. If anything, women in these ethnic cultures are often *more* heavily policed with respect to their sexual behavior. But European fantasies such as *Carmen* project license on to women of other races and classes. Given Rosi's decision to remain faithful to the libretto and score, he reinscribes some of these stereotypes, even as he overturns others. The only solution would be to abandon the text or rewrite it substantially, a solution he denies himself. What he can do – and does do magnificently – is to expose *Carmen*'s contradictions.

Rosi's production is filled with details that invite us to reread this familiar text. In the opening scene of Act I, for instance, he makes the intersection between class and sexual privilege explicit, as the soldiers practice a prurient form of surveillance from their high-rise quarters. They act like vultures, swooping down to surround and harass the innocent Micaëla, who barely escapes their clutches. The threat of gang rape hovers over this opening scene, and its menace continues to be felt when Zuniga uses military field-glasses to spy on women bathing or whenever the soldiers intrude into gypsy spaces demanding sexual favors.

Within this context, Carmen's self-possessed defiance takes on the weight of expressly political resistance. She exploits the few strategies available to her to practice sedition for the entire community: indeed, in both Acts II and III, the other gypsies speak openly of how her talents for enticing and distracting the enemy are indispensable to their collective ventures. Her initial seduction of José during the "Seguidilla" is clearly an instance of Carmen at work, preserving herself through whatever means she has.

Rosi's casting of Julia Migenes-Johnson in the title role contributes profoundly to his success in overturning received meanings. She is smaller and has a far lighter voice than the typical Carmen, and thus seems less the hefty *femme fatale* than a vivacious, independent young woman. Her sensuality is frank and joyful, not sinister. Moreover, she stands firm against José's demands, but yet struggles for survival all the way to the end. She does not sacrifice herself to fate. That the plot demands that *any* woman in that narrative space – even someone as vibrant as Migenes-Johnson – be exterminated calls into question more than ever the sexual politics of this opera. And Rosi makes this clear.

Hammerstein, Saura, Brook and Rosi ask us to rethink fundamentally what we thought we knew about *Carmen*, to experience ambiguities and contradictions in an opera that sometimes seems overfamiliar. In doing so, they have made it an artwork of the late twentieth century. And the puzzle of Bizet's masterpiece will pass on, still unresolved, to future generations.

Notes

1 Mérimée's *Carmen*

1 The first real review article appears only in 1852 and that in reference to a new edition of Mérimée stories. See Maurice Parturier's introduction to his edition of *Carmen* in P. Mérimée, *Contes et nouvelles* (Paris, 1967), vol. 2, p. 343. Further page numbers refer to this edition.

2 There are, however, many associations attached to the Latin word (and Mérimée invokes knowledge of Latin from the very beginning of the tale). The word denotes in Latin, among other things, song, prophecy, incantation, charm. In addition, a homonymic connection links the word to *carmin*, the color red. All of these associations will occur to the educated reader of the time as the story unfolds, and all of them resonate with important dimensions of the story. Throughout the story Carmen is always associated with the color red, the color not only of the life force itself, but, also, when spilled and thus on the outside, the color of death.

3 The Greek scholar appreciates the play on words between *thalamos* and *thanatos* that informs the original quotation.

4 In French this word means both basin and pelvis.

5 The only other time Mérimée specifically invokes a "woman's world" in the text, he does so in exactly the same manner. When Don José recalls going to the cigar factory to investigate the disturbance, he says that men are kept out of the factory at all times because it is hot there and the women work semiclothed. Clearly, it is only the physical aspect of their bodies that is of interest. Such seminudity is seen to be extremely threatening, as surely it would induce action on the part of men that they could not control.

6 Parturier, for instance, suggests that Mérimée needed to pad a slim story or perhaps wanted to show off his linguistic knowledge (Mérimée, *Contes*, p. 342). See also A. W. Raitt, *Prosper Mérimée* (London, 1970). Raitt calls it a "deliberate and provocative anticlimax" (p. 197) without further explanation.

7 It is important to note that this story appeared at a time when French women were beginning to assert themselves more forcefully. George Sand, the most visible feminist of the period, had been a major contributor to *La Revue des deux mondes*. In 1844, François Buloz, the editor of the review, dropped her because her novels were now said to be too "political" and not sufficiently "literary." Mérimée's tale is part of

147

the assault against emancipated women and seems always to have had renewed popularity at moments of renewed feminist activity.

2   The genesis of Bizet's *Carmen*

1 Quoted in Winton Dean, *Georges Bizet: His Life and Work* (London, 1965), p. 80. Bizet could be brutal about this sacred cow. In a letter to his mother-in-law Mme Halévy, he reported:

> Listen: one day, in front of [Ludovic] Halévy, I was expounding some rather subversive theories about *La Dame blanche*. I spoke the simple truth. "It is a loathsome opera, without talent, with no ideas, no *esprit*, no melodic invention, no anything whatsoever in the world, It is stupid, stupid, stupid!" Halévy, turning toward me with his sly smile, said (I have a witness): "Well, yes! You are right. Its success is incomprehensible; it is no good. *Only, you mustn't say so.*"

Quoted in Mina Curtiss, *Bizet and his World* (New York, 1958), p. 313, original emphasis. On the day of Bizet's funeral, the scheduled performance of *Carmen* was replaced by *La Dame blanche*.

2 Letter to Edmond Galabert, June 17, 1872. Quoted in Dean, *Georges Bizet*, p. 100.

3 For a complete account of the sources for *Carmen*, see Winton Dean, "Bizet's Self-Borrowings," *Music and Letters* 41 (1960), pp. 238–44.

4 As quoted in Curtiss, *Bizet and his World*, p. 373.

5 See Curtiss, *Bizet and his World*. Both Geneviève Halévy Bizet and her mother suffered from the kinds of vague nervous disorders prevalent among intelligent but confined upper-class women in the late nineteenth century. After Bizet's death, Geneviève married the lawyer Emile Straus and later became a friend of Marcel Proust. She served as the model for Proust's Duchesse de Guermantes. Curtiss was researching Proust when she stumbled upon the family records that inform her study of Bizet.

6 Ludovic Halévy, "La Millième Représentation de *Carmen*," *Le Théâtre* 145 (1905). A partial translation of the report is available in English as "Breaking the Rules," trans. Clarence H. Russell, *Opera News* 51, no. 13 (1987), pp. 36–7, 47.

7 As quoted in Curtiss, *Bizet and his World*, p. 379.

8 Pierre Berton, *Souvenirs de la vie de théâtre* (Paris, 1913), p. 239. As quoted in Curtiss, *Bizet and his World*, pp. 379–80.

9 Albert de Maugny, *Le Demi-Monde sous le Second Empire* (Paris, n.d.), p. 196. As quoted in Curtiss, *Bizet and his World*, p. 355. Winton Dean thinks it "inconceivable that Offenbach's soubrette Zulma Bouffar was his first choice for the heroine," though he does not elaborate. See his "The True 'Carmen?,'" *The Musical Times* 106 (1965), p. 854.

10 Letter of September 7, 1873. As quoted in Curtiss, *Bizet and his World*, p. 355.

11 Halévy, "La Millième Représentation," as quoted in Curtiss, *Bizet and his World*, pp. 381–2.

12 As quoted in Curtiss, *Bizet and his World*, p. 382.

13 See Evan Baker, "The Scene Designs for the First Performances of Georges Bizet's *Carmen*," *19th-Century Music* 13, no. 3 (1990), pp. 230–42.

14 Fritz Oeser, ed., *Carmen, Kritische Neuausgabe nach den Quellen* (Kassel, 1964).

15 Winton Dean, "The True 'Carmen?,'" pp. 846–55; "The Corruption of Carmen: The Perils of Pseudo-Musicology," *Musical Newsletter* 3 (1973), pp. 7–12, 20; Lesley A. Wright, "A New Source for *Carmen*," *19th-Century Music* 2, no. 1 (1978), pp. 61–71.

16 Vincent d'Indy, as quoted in Curtiss, *Bizet and his World*, p. 388.

17 Halévy, "La Millième Représentation," in "Breaking the Rules," pp. 36–7.

18 Massenet, letter of March 4, 1875, and Saint-Saëns, undated letter from about a week after the premiere. Both as quoted in Curtiss, *Bizet and his World*, pp. 395–6.

19 Jacques-Emile Blanche, *More Portraits of a Lifetime: 1918–1938* (London, 1939), pp. 156–7. As quoted in Curtiss, *Bizet and his World*, p. 391.

3 Images of race, class and gender in nineteenth-century French culture

1 See Edward Said, *Orientalism* (New York, 1979).

2 See James Creech, "Others," in *A New History of French Literature*, ed. Denis Hollier (Cambridge, Mass., 1989), pp. 409–15.

3 Christopher Miller, "Orientalism, Colonialism," in *A New History*, p. 698. See also Said, *Orientalism*, and Rana Kabbani, *Europe's Myths of the Orient* (Bloomington, Ind., 1986).

4 Victor Hugo, preface to *Les Orientales*, my translation. Similarly, Schlegel wrote: "We must seek the supreme Romanticism in the Orient," quoted in Raymond Schwab, *The Oriental Renaissance*, trans. Gene Patterson-Black and Victor Reinking (New York, 1984), p. 13.

5 Concerning the women of Cairo, Gérard de Nerval wrote: "Let us stay and try to raise a corner of that austere veil which the goddess of Saïs wears . . . From behind that rampart, ardent eyes await you, with all the seductions they can borrow from art" (*Voyage en Orient*, quoted in Miller, "Orientalism," p. 702). The French interest in penetrating behind the veil inspired a special genre of sexually provocative postcards. See Malek Alloula, *The Colonial Harem*, trans. Myrna Godzich and Wlad Godzich (Minneapolis, 1986).

6 Marianne Torgovnick, *Gone Primitive: Savage Intellects, Modern Lives* (Chicago, 1990), p. 157. The book juxtaposes such fantasies with the reality of exploitation and genocide.

7 Nelly Furman, "The Languages of Love in *Carmen*," in *Reading Opera*, ed. Arthur Groos and Roger Parker (Princeton, 1988), p. 169.

8 See the chart in Danièle Pistone, "Les Conditions historiques de l'exotisme musical français," *Revue internationale de la musique française* 6 (1981), p. 22.

9 Carl Dahlhaus, *Nineteenth-Century Music*, trans. J. Bradford Robinson (Berkeley and Los Angeles, 1989), p. 304. After explaining that "the nineteenth-century fashion for exoticism was partly motivated by the fact that colonialism ... became a national ideology with obvious implications for literature," he continues: "However, the crucial factor in the spread of exoticism among serious-minded musicians was a development in compositional technique: just as functional meter disintegrated into 'musical prose,' functional harmony began to give way to coloristic harmony" (p. 304). Musical exoticism remains a formal issue for Dahlhaus.

10 The colonies were beginning to send back to France persons of foreign racial stock, but when *Carmen* was written, the chief models for the Other-at-home remained gypsies and Jews.

11 See Jerrold Seigel, *Bohemian Paris: Culture, Politics, and the Boundaries of Bourgeois Life, 1830–1930* (New York, 1986).

12 Concerning the attractions of the bohemian underworld for Baudelaire, Seigel writes: "He loved the city for its bandits and prostitutes, its 'monstrosities blooming like a flower,' because every departure from the norms of ordinary life opened up a space where the imagination could expand to its own limits" (*Bohemian Paris*, p. 108). Baudelaire's imagery is strikingly like that of Hugo's; both resonate with the allure of female sexuality. Seigel also explains that "Bohemia was less a genuine departure from the ground of bourgeois experience than accentuation of certain of its features; the tension between work and indulgence, *travail* and *jouissance*, was part of bourgeois life, too" (p. 123).

13 See Sandra M. Gilbert and Susan Gubar, *The Madwoman in the Attic: The Woman Writer and the Nineteenth-Century Literary Imagination* (New Haven, 1979), pp. 20–7; Nancy Armstrong, *Desire and Domestic Fiction: A Political History of the Novel* (Oxford, 1987); Peter Gay, *The Bourgeois Experience: Victoria to Freud, I: Education of the Senses* (Oxford, 1984); and Bram Dijkstra, *Idols of Perversity: Fantasies of Feminine Evil in Fin-de-Siècle Culture* (Oxford, 1986). These document both the cloying images of domesticity from the first half of the century and the monstrous ones that emerge when women start to refuse that role.

14 Letter to Edmond Galabert, October 1867. As quoted in Curtiss, *Bizet and his World*, p. 206.

15 Gay, *The Bourgeois Experience*, p. 169.

16 *Ibid.*, p. 193. See also Sander L. Gilman, *Difference and Pathology: Stereotypes of Sexuality, Race, and Madness* (Ithaca, N.Y., 1985); and Dijkstra, *Idols of Perversity*.

17 Letter to Edmond Galabert (1868), as quoted in Dean, *Georges Bizet*, p. 60.

18 See Charles Bernheimer, *Figures of Ill Repute: Representing Prostitution in Nineteenth-Century France* (Cambridge, Mass., 1989), pp. 1–33.

19 *Ibid.*, pp. 160–3. Halévy was regarded as such an expert in this area that Zola consulted with him while writing *Nana* (Bernheimer, p. 230).

20 See Curtiss, *Bizet and his World*, pp. 165–71.

21 *Ibid.*, p. 169.
22 *Ibid.*, pp. 170–1.
23 Bernheimer, *Figures of Ill Repute*, p. 88.
24 Besides Bernheimer, see Gilman, "The Hottentot and the Prostitute" and "Black Sexuality and Modern Consciousness," in *Difference and Pathology*, pp. 76–127.
25 Quoted in Bernheimer, *Figures of Ill Repute*, p. 52.
26 Bernheimer, *Figures of Ill Repute*, pp. 69–88 and 200–33.
27 See the comparison between Romanticism and Realism in Ross Chambers, "Literature Deterritorialized," in *A New History of French Literature*, pp. 710–16. See also Carl Dahlhaus, *Realism in Nineteenth-Century Music*, trans. Mary Whittall (Cambridge, 1985). Dahlhaus' arguments are motivated by his desire to dismantle the specter of Soviet "socialist realism."
28 See Elaine Showalter, *The Female Malady: Women, Madness, and English Culture, 1830–1980* (New York, 1987).
29 See Gilman, *Difference and Pathology*; and Klaus Theweleit, *Male Fantasies, I: Women, Floods, Bodies, History*, trans. Stephen Conway (Minneapolis, 1987).
30 Edouard Drumont, "Le Monde de Murget," *La Libre Parole* (June 26, 1985), as quoted in Seigel, *Bohemian Paris*, p. 180.

4 The musical languages of *Carmen*

1 I am drawing here on models of criticism developed by Mikhail Bakhtin. See *The Dialogic Imagination*, trans. Caryl Emerson and Michael Holquist (Austin, Texas, 1981). For dialogic readings of instrumental music, see Lawrence Kramer, *Music as Cultural Practice, 1800–1900* (Berkeley and Los Angeles, 1990); and Susan McClary, "A Dialectic from the Enlightenment: Mozart's *Piano Concerto in G Major, K. 453*, Movement 2," *Cultural Critique* 4 (1986), pp. 129–69; and "Narrative Agendas in 'Absolute' Music: Identity and Difference in Brahms's Third Symphony," in *Music and Difference*, ed. Ruth Solie (Berkeley and Los Angeles, forthcoming).
2 Quoted in Dean, *Georges Bizet: His Life and Work*, p. 107.
3 Quoted in Curtiss, *Bizet and his World*, p. 390.
4 Dean, *Georges Bizet*, p. 22.
5 Letter to Paul Lacombe (March 1867), quoted in Dean, *Georges Bizet*, p. 240.
6 Review of *Djamileh*, quoted in Curtiss, *Bizet and his World*, p. 325. For discussions of Wagnerism in France, see Richard Sieburth, "The Music of the Future," in *A New History of French Literature*, ed. Denis Hollier (Cambridge, Mass., 1989), pp. 789–98, and David C. Large and William Weber, *Wagnerism in European Culture and Politics* (Ithaca, N.Y., 1984).
7 Letter from Rome to his mother, quoted in Dean, *Georges Bizet*, p. 46.
8 Letter to Mme. Halévy (1871), quoted in Dean, *ibid.*, pp. 90–1.
9 Quoted in Curtiss, *Bizet and his World*, p. 107.
10 Letter to Mme. Halévy (1871), quoted in Dean, *Georges Bizet*, p. 91.

11 Dean, *Georges Bizet*, throughout the discussions of music.

12 Review by Benjamin Jouvin, *Figaro* (1863), quoted in Curtiss, *Bizet and his World*, p. 139.

13 Théophile Gautier, review of *La Jolie Fille de Perth*, *Le Moniteur universel* (1866), quoted in Curtiss, *Bizet and his World*, p. 211.

14 Dean, *Georges Bizet*, p. 38.

15 Carl Dahlhaus, *Nineteenth-Century Music*, p. 280.

16 Elaine Brody, *Paris: The Musical Kaleidoscope, 1870–1925* (New York, 1987), p. 72.

17 Curtiss, *Bizet and his World*, p. 170. The inventory of Bizet's library reveals that he owned five songs by Yradier (p. 474).

18 Achille de Lauzières de Thémines, *La Patrie* (March 8, 1875), quoted in Curtiss, *Bizet and his World*, p. 401.

19 Alphonse Daudet, quoted in Curtiss, *ibid.*, p. 333.

20 Ernest Reyer, quoted in Curtiss, *ibid.*, pp. 325–6.

21 Dahlhaus, *Nineteenth-Century Music*, p. 306.

22 Gautier, Curtiss, *Bizet and his World*, pp. 211–12.

23 Gautier, *Voyage pittoresque en Algérie* (1845), as quoted in Alloula, *The Colonial Harem*, p. 85.

24 For more of the ways fear of the body informs Western music and musicology, see McClary, *Feminine Endings: Music, Gender, and Sexuality* (Minneapolis, 1991).

25 In *Ivan IV*, Bizet has a male character sing the principal Orientalist number, a serenade. Ivan dismisses the serenade by declaring such music suitable only for women. Even when put into the mouths of men, this discourse is understood as essentially feminine, as was the "Orient" itself. See Chapter 3.

26 My position here differs markedly from Dahlhaus': "As an opera heroine, Carmen is characterized basically by a negative trait: she is incapable of attaining lyric urgency. Carmen can parody lyricism . . . but she cannot make it her own." *Nineteenth-Century Music*, p. 282.

27 For more on the dread of mass culture in the late nineteenth century and its association with the "feminine," see Andreas Huyssen, "Mass Culture as Woman: Modernism's Other," in *After the Great Divide: Modernism, Mass Culture, Postmodernism* (Bloomington, Ind., 1986), pp. 44–64. For discussion of the *café-concerts*, see Jacques Attali, *Noise*, trans. Brian Massumi (Minneapolis, 1985), pp. 72–7; and Brody, *Paris*, pp. 97–111.

28 Arnold Schoenberg, *Theory of Harmony*, trans. Roy E. Carter (Berkeley and Los Angeles, 1983), p. 129.

5 Synopsis and analysis

1 An early version of the score set this dialogue as a *mélodrame*, with an ironic canon based on the children's march played between solo violin and cello. Winton Dean argues that Bizet eliminated this before the premiere, although Fritz Oeser restores it in his critical score. See Dean, "The True 'Carmen?,'" pp. 849–50.

2 In the first draft (reinscribed in Oeser's score), the male chorus injects a

plea for the women to respond to them, and then the women repeat their chorus, creating the anticipated ABA form. Bizet introduced major cuts into this act during rehearsals, thus streamlining the action. Carmen's advent is less disruptive if the cigarette chorus is permitted to round off.

3 See Wright, "A New Source for *Carmen*," pp. 63–4.

4 In early drafts of the opera, this duel/duet was quite extensive. Oeser includes all of it in his critical score, although Dean argues convincingly that Bizet himself shortened the scene during rehearsals before the premiere. See "The True 'Carmen?,'" p. 848.

5 Bizet produced several versions of the ending before settling on this one. Once again, Oeser's score records a version that had been rejected by the time of the premiere. See Dean's discussion of the differences in "The True 'Carmen?,'" pp. 850–2.

6 The reception of *Carmen*

1 Curtiss, *Bizet and his World*, p. 395.

2 Quoted in Dean, *Georges Bizet*, p. 116. Curtiss comments that "[Bizet] learned quickly, with breathtaking impact, that the process of launching a revolution more or less singlehanded was not enjoyable" (*Bizet and his World*, p. 397).

3 Jean-Pierre-Oscar Comettant (*Le Siècle*), quoted in Curtiss, *ibid.*, pp. 403–4.

4 Achille de Lauzières (*Le Patrie*), quoted in Curtiss, *ibid.*, pp. 399–400.

5 Comettant, as quoted in Curtiss, *ibid.*, p. 404.

6 Théodore de Banville (*Le National*), quoted in Curtiss, *ibid.*, p. 408.

7 Bizet, quoted in Curtiss, *ibid.*, p. 408.

8 Léon Escudier, as quoted in Dean, *Georges Bizet*, p. 118.

9 Baudouin (*La République française*), quoted in Dean, *ibid.*, p. 118.

10 Arthur Pougin, quoted in Dean, *ibid.*, p. 117.

11 Banville, quoted in Curtiss, *Bizet and his World*, p. 409.

12 Ernest Reyer (*Le Journal des débats*), quoted in Curtiss, *ibid.*, pp. 433–4.

13 Adolphe Jullien (*Le Français*), quoted in Dean, *Georges Bizet*, p. 120.

14 This statement first appears in Friedrich Wilhelm Langhans, *Die Geschichte der Musik des 17. 18. und 19. Jahrhunderts*, vol. 2 (Leipzig, 1887), p. 536. It is repeated in John W. Klein, "Bizet and Wagner," *Music and Letters* 28 (1947), pp. 59–61, along with other bits of information, most of which are not clearly documented. Klein also reports that Wagner liked best the Micaëla–José duet, which he would have the pianist Joseph Rubinstein play for him, and that Wagner and Cosima later became quite ambivalent about *Carmen*.

15 Andrew de Ternant, "Debussy and Brahms," *The Musical Times*, 65 (1924), p. 609.

16 David Brown, *Tchaikovsky: The Crisis Years, 1874–1878* (New York, 1983), p. 58.

17 See his program to the Fourth Symphony in Brown, *Tchaikovsky*, pp. 163–6.

18 Friedrich Nietzsche, *The Case of Wagner*, trans. Walter Kaufmann (New York, 1967). pp. 157–9.

19 Review, *Observer*, quoted in Dennis Arundell, *The Critic at the Opera* (London, 1957), p. 359.

20 George Bernard Shaw, "Twenty Years Too Late," *The World* (May 30, 1894). Reprinted in *Shaw's Music*, vol. 3, ed. Dan H. Laurence (New York, 1981), p. 225. For Shaw's horrified account of the death scene, see below.

21 See, for instance, Wallace Brockway and Herbert Weinstock, *The Opera: A History of its Creation and Performance, 1600–1941* (New York, 1941), pp. 289–301. For a critique of *Carmen*'s vaunted perfection, see George R. Marek, "*Carmen* – The 'Perfect Opera,'" in his *Opera as Theater* (New York, 1962), pp. 105–8.

22 Donald Jay Grout, *A Short History of Opera*, 2nd edn. (New York, 1965), p. 427.

23 Ernest Newman, *More Opera Nights* (London, 1954), p. 433.

24 Brockway and Weinstock, *The Opera*, p. 297.

25 Herbert Graf, *Opera for the People* (Minneapolis, 1951).

26 Herbert Lindenberger, *Opera, the Extravagant Art* (Ithaca, N.Y., 1984), p. 203.

27 Dahlhaus, *Realism in Nineteenth-Century Music*, pp. 89 and 92. See also his *Nineteenth-Century Music*, pp. 280–2.

28 Jullien, quoted in Dean, *Georges Bizet*, p. 120. Dean is astounded by this statement.

29 Shaw, "Twenty Years Too Late," p. 226.

30 Frederick H. Martens, *A Thousand and One Nights of Opera* (New York, 1926), p. 440.

31 Catherine Clément, *Opera, or the Undoing of Women*, trans. Betsy Wing (Minneapolis, 1988), pp. 49–50.

32 Michel Leiris, *Manhood: A Journey from Childhood into the Fierce Order of Virility*, trans. Richard Howard (San Francisco, 1984), p. 54. *Manhood* was written after Leiris' advances were spurned by an African showgirl, to which Leiris responded first by threatening to castrate himself and then by producing this book.

33 Paul Bekker, *The Changing Opera*, trans. Arthur Mendel (New York, 1935), pp. 227–9.

34 For more on the appeal of female corpses in late nineteenth-century and present-day culture, see Elaine Showalter, *Sexual Anarchy: Gender and Culture at the Fin de Siècle* (New York, 1990), especially Chapter 7.

35 See McClary, "Living to Tell: Madonna's Resurrection of the Fleshly," in *Feminine Endings: Music, Gender, and Sexuality*, pp. 148–66.

36 Clément, *Opera*, p. 59. A common complaint about Clément's book is that it neglects dealing with the music itself. For a sustained argument concerning musical procedures and the "necessary" purging of the feminine element, see my *Feminine Endings*.

37 Nelly Furman, "The Languages of Love in *Carmen*," pp. 168–83.

7   *Carmen* on film

1 See Graf, *Opera for the People*, pp. 209–10.
2 Jeremy Tambling, *Opera, Ideology and Film* (New York, 1987), pp. 25–9.
3 *Kamikaze Hearts* problematizes what it means for women to participate in the production of exploitative representations – representations for which they are financially rewarded, but which may finally so thoroughly influence their own sense of self that their identities become fused with the glamorous surfaces they have learned to fabricate. While it depicts explicit sexual activity, this film may be closer to the antipornographic *This Is Not a Love Story* than to films (or operas) designed for titillation.
4 I am excluding Jean-Luc Godard's *Prénom Carmen* (also 1984), because Godard tries to distance the story from Bizet's music by counterposing Beethoven quartets to the action.
5 Oscar Hammerstein II, *Carmen Jones* (New York, 1945), pp. xiii–xv.
6 *Ibid.*, p. xviii. As further justification, he points out that "Spanish music was deeply influenced by the Moors from Africa. The rhythm of the 'Habañera' is even closer to the home of Carmen Jones. It is a West Indian rhythm exported to Spain, heard and imitated by Bizet." He then hastens to add, "I mention these academic facts without being very much impressed by them myself. My belief about words and music is that when a melody is good to hear, it can take on any color the lyric gives it" (p. xviii).
7 David Wills has criticized the sexual politics of this film:

> [Saura's Carmen] is not presented as a demimondaine, but rather as an independent young woman. However, the narrative develops to cast her in more or less the same mold as that nineteenth-century Carmen, as cruel and treacherous, as having spoiled the innocence of an encounter and having toyed with the emotions of her partner, as contaminating and castrating. When her dance-master murders her . . . one may read as pitiful his inability to respond to her assertion of independence with anything other than the violence of possessiveness, but I think one must also read a very classical form of vengeance or punishment meted out since time immemorial to the sexually unfaithful woman.
> "Carmen: Sound/Effect," *Cinema Journal* 25, no. 4 (1986), p. 35.

8 Quoted in Glenn Loney, "The Carmen Connection," *Opera News* 48, no. 3 (1983), p. 12.
9 Of the three film versions of Brook's production, I am treating the one with Hélène Delavault as Carmen.
10 Constant "'treated the music as though it were lieder,' Brook explains. [He] 'found the music not bombastic, as it is often played, but like a Debussy or a Duparc song.'" Loney, "The Carmen Connection," p. 14.
11 Wills, "Carmen: Sound/Effect," p. 34. Likewise Tambling writes: "[Brook] believes in the tragedy as Mérimée wrote it; rather than as Bizet presented it, but does not wish to inspect what underlies the Mérimée text, to see where it is coming from; accepts it rather, and merely wishes not to romanticize a prostitute, as Carmen very clearly is in his Act II" (*Opera*, p. 35).

12 For an account of Rosi's career, see Michel Ciment, "Rosi in a New Key," *American Film* 9, no. 10 (1984), pp. 37–42. Elsewhere Rosi explains that "I believe I would not have agreed to make another opera ... this is one of the rare realist operas that exist." Quoted in Jean-Michel Brèque, "Réaliste et lyrique: Carmen dans sa vérite," *Positif* 278 (1984), p. 14, my translation.

13 Tambling, *Opera*, pp. 35–6.

14 Ciment, "Rosi in a New Key," p. 39. Ciment comments: "Rosi's investigative films are like tools to understand an evil reality and to avoid adopting a fatalistic view of life" (p. 42).

Bibliography

Alloula, Malek, *The Colonial Harem*, trans. Myrna Godzich and Wlad Godzich. Minneapolis, 1986.

Armstrong, Nancy, *Desire and Domestic Fiction: A Political History of the Novel*. Oxford, 1987.

Attali, Jacques, *Noise*, trans. Brian Massumi. Minneapolis, 1985.

Baker, Evan, "The Scene Designs for the First Performances of Georges Bizet's *Carmen*." *19th-Century Music* 13, no. 3 (1990), pp. 230–42.

Bakhtin, Mikhail, *The Dialogic Imagination*, trans. Caryl Emerson and Michael Holquist. Austin, Texas, 1981.

Bekker, Paul, *The Changing Opera*, trans. Arthur Mendel. New York, 1935.

Bernheimer, Charles, *Figures of Ill Repute: Representing Prostitution in Nineteenth-Century France*. Cambridge, Mass., 1989.

Bizet, Georges, *Lettres, impressions de Rome, 1857–60, la commune, 1871*. Ed. Louis Ganderax. Paris, 1907.

"Unpublished Letters by Georges Bizet." Ed. Mina Curtiss. *Musical Quarterly* 36 (1950), pp. 375–409.

Brèque, Jean-Michel, "Réaliste et lyrique: Carmen dans sa vérité." *Positif* 278 (1984), pp. 13–18.

Brockway, Wallace, and Herbert Weinstock, *The Opera: A History of its Creation and Performance, 1600–1941*. New York, 1941.

Brody, Elaine, *Paris: The Musical Kaleidoscope, 1870–1925*. New York, 1987.

Brown, David, *Tchaikovsky: The Crisis Years, 1874–1878*. New York, 1983.

Cardoze, Michel, *Georges Bizet*. Paris, 1982.

Chambers, Ross, "Literature Deterritorialized." In *A New History of French Literature*, ed. Denis Hollier (Cambridge, Mass., 1989), pp. 710–16.

Ciment, Michel, "Rosi in a New Key." *American Film* 9, no. 10 (1984), pp. 37–42.

Clément, Catherine, *Opera, or the Undoing of Women*, trans. Betsy Wing. Minneapolis, 1988.

Creech, James, "Others." In *A New History of French Literature*, ed. Hollier, pp. 409–15.

Curtiss, Mina, *Bizet and his World*. New York, 1958.

Dahlhaus, Carl, *Nineteenth-Century Music*, trans. J. Bradford Robinson. Berkeley and Los Angeles, 1989.

Realism in Nineteenth-Century Music, trans. Mary Whittall. Cambridge, 1985.

157

Dean, Winton, "Bizet's Self-Borrowings." *Music and Letters* 41 (1960), pp. 238–44.

"The Corruption of Carmen: The Perils of Pseudo-Musicology." *Musical Newsletter* 3 (1973), pp. 7–12, 20.

Georges Bizet: His Life and Work. London, 1965.

"The True 'Carmen?.'" *The Musical Times* 106 (1965), pp. 846–55.

Dijkstra, Bram, *Idols of Perversity: Fantasies of Feminine Evil in Fin-de-Siècle Culture.* Oxford, 1986.

Fulcher, Jane, *The Nation's Image: French Grand Opera as Politics and Politicized Art* (Cambridge, 1987).

Furman, Nelly, "The Languages of Love in *Carmen.*" In *Reading Opera*, ed. Arthur Groos and Roger Parker (Princeton, 1988), pp. 168–83.

Gay, Peter, *The Bourgeois Experience: Victoria to Freud, I: Education of the Senses.* Oxford, 1984.

Gilbert, Sandra M., and Susan Gubar, *The Madwoman in the Attic: The Woman Writer and the Nineteenth-Century Literary Imagination.* New Haven, 1979.

Gilman, Sander L., *Difference and Pathology: Stereotypes of Sexuality, Race, and Madness.* Ithaca, N.Y., 1985.

Graf, Herbert, *Opera for the People.* Minneapolis, 1951.

Grout, Donald Jay, *A Short History of Opera*, 2nd edn. New York, 1965.

Halévy, Ludovic, "La Millième Représentation de *Carmen.*" *Le Théâtre* 145 (1905). For partial translation, see Russell, Clarence H.

Hammerstein, Oscar, II, *Carmen Jones.* New York, 1945.

Hollier, Denis, ed., *A New History of French Literature.* Cambridge, Mass., 1989.

Huebner, Steven, "Paris Opera Audiences, 1830–1870." *Music and Letters* 70 (1989), pp. 203–56.

Hugo, Victor, *Les Orientales* (1829). Ed. Pierre Albouy. Paris, 1966.

Huyssen, Andreas, *After the Great Divide: Modernism, Mass Culture, Postmodernism.* Bloomington, Ind., 1986.

Kabbani, Rana, *Europe's Myths of the Orient.* Bloomington, Ind., 1986.

Klein, John W., "Bizet and Wagner." *Music and Letters* 28 (1947), pp. 50–62.

"Bizet's Admirers and Detractors." *Music and Letters* 19 (1938), pp. 405–16.

Kramer, Lawrence, *Music as Cultural Practice, 1800–1900.* Berkeley and Los Angeles, 1990.

Large, David C., and William Weber, *Wagnerism in European Culture and Politics.* Ithaca, N.Y., 1984.

Leiris, Michel, *Manhood: A Journey from Childhood into the Fierce Order of Virility*, trans. Richard Howard. San Francisco, 1984.

Lindenberger, Herbert, *Opera, The Extravagant Art.* Ithaca, N.Y., 1984.

Loney, Glenn, "The Carmen Connection." *Opera News* 48, no. 3 (1983), pp. 10–14.

McClary, Susan, *Feminine Endings: Music, Gender, and Sexuality.* Minneapolis, 1991.

Maingueneau, Dominique, *Carmen: les racines d'un mythe.* Paris, 1984.

"Signification du décor: l'exemple de *Carmen.*" *Romantisme* 38 (1982), pp. 87–91.

Marek, George R., *Opera as Theater*. New York, 1962.

Martens, Frederick H., *A Thousand and One Nights of Opera*. New York, 1926.

Mérimée, Prosper, *Contes et nouvelles*. Paris, 1967.

Miller, Christopher L., "Orientalism, Colonialism." In *A New History of French Literature*, ed. Hollier, pp. 698–705.

Moser, Françoise, *Vie et aventures de Céleste Mogador*. Paris, 1935.

Newman, Ernest, *More Opera Nights*. London, 1954.

Nietzsche, Friedrich, *The Case of Wagner*, trans. Walter Kaufmann. New York, 1967.

Oeser, Fritz, ed., *Carmen, kritische Neuausgabe nach den Quellen*. Kassel, 1964.

Pistone, Danièle, "Les Conditions historiques de l'exotisme musical français." *Revue internationale de la musique française* 6 (1981), pp. 11–22.

Raitt, A. W., *Prosper Mérimée*. London, 1970.

Roy, Jean, *Bizet*. Paris, 1983.

Russell, Clarence H., "Breaking the Rules." *Opera News* 51, no. 13 (1987), pp. 36–7, 47.

Said, Edward, *Orientalism*. New York, 1979.

Schoenberg, Arnold, *Theory of Harmony*, trans. Roy E. Carter. Berkeley and Los Angeles, 1983.

Schwab, Raymond, *The Oriental Renaissance*, trans. Gene Patterson-Black and Victor Reinking. New York, 1984.

Seigel, Jerrold, *Bohemian Paris: Culture, Politics, and the Boundaries of Bourgeois Life, 1830–1930*. New York, 1986.

Shaw, George Bernard, "Twenty Years Too Late." In *Shaw's Music*, vol. 3, ed. Dan H. Laurence (New York, 1981), pp. 222–8.

Showalter, Elaine, *The Female Malady: Women, Madness, and English Culture, 1830–1980*. New York, 1987.

Sexual Anarchy: Gender and Culture at the Fin de Siècle. New York, 1990.

Sieburth, Richard, "The Music of the Future." In *A New History of French Literature*, ed. Hollier, pp. 789–98.

Tambling, Jeremy, *Opera, Ideology and Film*. New York, 1987.

Tchaikovsky, Peter Illych, reactions to *Carmen*: see Brown, David.

Ternant, Andrew de, "Debussy and Brahms." *The Musical Times* 65 (1924), pp. 608–9.

Theweleit, Klaus, *Male Fantasies, I: Women, Floods, Bodies, History*, trans. Stephen Conway. Minneapolis, 1987.

Tiersot, Julien, "Bizet and Spanish Music." *Musical Quarterly* 13 (1927), pp. 566–81.

Torgovnick, Marianne, *Gone Primitive: Savage Intellects, Modern Lives*. Chicago, 1990.

Tuten, Frederic, "Tor-re-a-dora, Blood-up-on-the-Floor-a: Peter Brook's 'Carmen.'" *Artforum* 20, no. 10 (1982), pp. 76–7.

Wills, David, "Carmen: Sound/Effect." *Cinema Journal* 25, no. 4 (1986), pp. 33–43.

Wright, Lesley A., "A New Source for *Carmen*." *19th-Century Music* 2, no. 1 (1978), pp. 61–71.

Index